CAMBRIDGE MUSIC HANDBOOKS

Beethoven: Violin Concerto

CAMBRIDGE MUSIC HANDBOOKS

GENERAL EDITOR Julian Rushton

Published titles

Bach: *The Brandenburg Concertos* MALCOLM BOYD
Bach: Mass in B Minor JOHN BUTT
Bartók: *Concerto for Orchestra* DAVID COOPER
Beethoven: *Missa solemnis* WILLIAM DRABKIN
Beethoven: *Pastoral Symphony* DAVID WYN JONES
Beethoven: Symphony No. 9 NICHOLAS COOK
Beethoven: Violin Concerto ROBIN STOWELL
Berg: Violin Concerto ANTHONY POPLE
Berlioz: *Roméo et Juliette* JULIAN RUSHTON
Brahms: *A German Requiem* MICHAEL MUSGRAVE
Brahms: Clarinet Quintet COLIN LAWSON
Brahms: Symphony No. 1 DAVID BRODBECK
Britten: *War Requiem* MERVYN COOKE
Chopin: The Four Ballades JIM SAMSON
Chopin: The Piano Concertos JOHN RINK
Debussy: *La mer* SIMON TREZISE
Gershwin: *Rhapsody in Blue* DAVID SCHIFF
Handel: *Messiah* DONALD BURROWS
Haydn: *The Creation* NICHOLAS TEMPERLEY
Haydn: String Quartets, Op. 50 W. DEAN SUTCLIFFE
Holst: *The Planets* RICHARD GREENE
Ives: *Concord Sonata* GEOFFREY BLOCK
Janáček: *Glagolitic Mass* PAUL WINGFIELD
Liszt: Sonata in B Minor KENNETH HAMILTON
Mahler: Symphony No. 3 PETER FRANKLIN
Mendelssohn: *The Hebrides* and other overtures R. LARRY TODD
Monteverdi: Vespers (1610) JOHN WHENHAM
Mozart: Clarinet Concerto COLIN LAWSON
Mozart: The 'Haydn' Quartets JOHN IRVING
Mozart: The 'Jupiter' Symphony ELAINE R. SISMAN
Musorgsky: *Pictures at an Exhibition* MICHAEL RUSS
Nielsen: Symphony No. 5 DAVID FANNING
Schoenberg: *Pierrot lunaire* JONATHAN DUNSBY
Schubert: *Die schöne Müllerin* SUSAN YOUENS
Schumann: Fantasie, Op. 17 NICHOLAS MARSTON
Sibelius: Symphony No. 5 JAMES HEPOKOSKI
Strauss: *Also sprach Zarathustra* JOHN WILLIAMSON
Stravinsky: *Oedipus rex* STEPHEN WALSH
The Beatles: *Sgt. Pepper's Lonely Hearts Club Band* ALLAN MOORE
Verdi: *Requiem* DAVID ROSEN
Vivaldi: *The Four Seasons* and other concertos, Op. 8 PAUL EVERETT

Beethoven: Violin Concerto

Robin Stowell

University of Wales, Cardiff

CAMBRIDGE UNIVERSITY PRESS
Cambridge, New York, Melbourne, Madrid, Cape Town, Singapore, São Paulo

Cambridge University Press
The Edinburgh Building, Cambridge CB2 2RU, UK

Published in the United States of America by Cambridge University Press, New York

www.cambridge.org
Information on this title: www.cambridge.org/9780521451598

First published 1998

A catalogue record for this publication is available from the British Library

ISBN-13   978-0-521-45159-8 hardback
ISBN-10   0-521-45159-0 hardback

ISBN-13   978-0-521-45775-0 paperback
ISBN-10   0-521-45775-0 paperback

Transferred to digital printing 2005

Contents

Contents

Figures

Preface

Beethoven's Violin Concerto, the 'King of Concertos', the *ne plus ultra* of fiddling ambition, occupies a place of such transcendent glory in the musical firmament that its eminence is seldom disputed. It has become customary to accept it as the unparalleled model of concerto construction, the keystone of the violin repertory. (Lawrence Sommers)[1]

Despite Sommers' extravagant prose, few would dissent from his assessment of Beethoven's masterpiece, the only major violin concerto composed between Mozart's five concertos of 1775 and Mendelssohn's E minor Concerto Op. 64 (1844). As a model of melodic invention, spaciousness of design, sheer clarity and logic of organisation, Beethoven's Concerto has gained a place in the repertory of 'every violinist, who aims at being more than the mere virtuoso' and 'has become the touchstone marking the maturity of the performing artist'.[3] In terms of the audio industry and the concert world in the current century, it has long stood in splendid isolation, so rare have been the opportunities to witness performances of other late-eighteenth- and early-nineteenth-century concertos, save perhaps Viotti's No. 22 in A minor or Spohr's No. 8 in A minor Op. 47 ('in modo di scena cantante').

Surprisingly, isolation of a less favourable kind coloured its early history. The present volume explores this concerto's background history, its genesis, its context in Beethoven's oeuvre, and the influences which combined in its conception. It traces how people reacted to the work in the musical press of Beethoven's time and on the concert

[1] Sommers, 'Beethoven's Violin Concerto', p. 46.
[2] J. Joachim and A. Moser, *Violinschule* (2 vols., Berlin, 1902–5) trans. A. Moffat (3 vols., Berlin and Leipzig, 1907), III, p. 181
[3] Moser, *Geschichte des Violinspiels*, p. 508.

platform during its first crucial years, and how it eventually entered the mainstream repertory, spawning numerous recordings and editions which reflect changing traditions of performance; and it examines the work's principal sources and many of its textual problems, including discussion of the adaptation for piano and orchestra, Op. 61a. Two chapters consider the structure and style of its three movements, and a final section reviews the wide variety of cadenzas that have been written to complement the concerto throughout its performance history.

I must acknowledge the assistance of a number of friends and colleagues who have helped to render this book more adequate than it might have been. Clive Brown, Jonathan Del Mar, Owen Jander and Peter Williams have all showed characteristic kindness in sharing relevant information, and the excellent work of Alan Tyson, the late Shin Augustinus Kojima and the late Boris Schwarz has also proved invaluable. Research for this volume was facilitated by a travel grant from the Department of Music, Cardiff University of Wales, and by the assistance readily given by Gill Jones and her colleagues in the Music Library at Cardiff University, to whom I offer my sincere thanks. Julian Rushton deserves special mention for his role as a patient, sympathetic and helpful series editor, not forgetting my copy-editor, Lucy Carolan, and the rest of Penny Souster's efficient team at Cambridge University Press who have seen the volume into print. Juliane Nau kindly assisted in the final stages with some German translation problems and, as always, my wife, Jane, and my family lent their encouragement and support throughout.

Study scores

The textual history of this concerto is so complex that it is difficult to recommend a convenient, and appropriate, 'all-purpose' score for the reader's use in conjunction with this handbook. The best-edited score to the late 1960s appears in the fourth volume (1863) of Breitkopf & Härtel's *L. van Beethovens Werke* (Leipzig, 1862–5). The editor is not named and there is no critical report. Based evidently on a comparison of the autograph MS and the first printed edition (Vienna, 1808) and incorporating numerous appropriate corrections, it is free of many of the errors included in most modern editions. Other pre-1960s editions that are not textually derived from the Breitkopf *Gesamtausgabe*, for example Wilhelm Altmann's miniature score for Eulenburg, should be used only with extreme caution, as they appear to be based only on the first printed edition and thus perpetuate significant errors. The most scholarly critical edition available as a miniature score is that by Alan Tyson (Eulenburg, *c*1967), which includes full documentation about the principal sources, correcting countless errors and suggesting numerous plausible solutions to textual problems. However, its plates are unfortunately those of such a corrupt score that several minor mistakes still remain. Preferable, therefore, is Shin Augustinus Kojima's edition which appears in volume III/4 of *L. van Beethoven: Werke: neue Ausgabe sämtlicher Werke* (Munich, 1973). Kojima's critical report remained in manuscript for some time – he left the Beethoven Archiv in March, 1979 to return to Japan – and was not published until 1994, eleven years after his death, in a revision by Ernst Herttrich. One of the progressive features of Kojima's report was a bar-for-bar musical comparison of the various versions of the concerto's solo violin part. Herttrich expands upon this imaginative idea in a thirty-page appendix which includes the so-called 'definitive version' centrally placed in each system of music; earlier versions of the solo line are printed above this, in a smaller typeface, while alternative readings which Beethoven did not definitively cancel from the autograph score appear below, also in smaller type.

1

Towards the Violin Concerto Op. 61

Beethoven's Violin Concerto in the context of his oeuvre

Beethoven began to make his mark as a composer during the 1790s. Apart from one visit to Vienna in 1787, when he met and impressed Mozart, family problems had virtually tied him to Bonn. In late 1792 he returned to Vienna, this time to stay. His ascendancy was rapid. His entry into Viennese social circles was eased by support gained from the Elector-Archbishop Maximilian Franz of Cologne, uncle of the Emperor Leopold II, and Count Waldstein. So, too, was his acceptance as a pupil of Joseph Haydn from late 1792 to 1793. More influential, however, were his studies in counterpoint with Albrechtsberger and his occasional instruction from the Imperial Kapellmeister Antonio Salieri. By the turn of the century his compositions had gained for him such prestige that he could write to Franz Wegeler, 'I am offered more commissions than it is possible for me to carry out...people no longer come to an arrangement with me, I state my price and they pay.'[1]

It has long been customary to divide Beethoven's oeuvre into three periods on the basis of style and chronology. Maynard Solomon, among others, has recently subjected this doctrine to close and sceptical scrutiny but has concluded that these periods are reinforced by many historical and stylistic factors, especially the significant changes in Beethoven's inner life, in his fundamental modes of patronage, and indeed in the Viennese Zeitgeist at large.[2] Vincent d'Indy labelled these periods 'Imitation' (to c1802), 'Externalisation' (c1802–c1816) and 'Reflection' (c1815–27),[3] the works of the first period naturally showing most clearly Beethoven's dependence on the Classical tradition.

Prompted by his 'Heiligenstadt Testament' letter of 6 October 1802, in which Beethoven movingly describes his feelings on realising that his deafness was incurable, his second period was one of reassessment, of emotional strain, of self-revelation and of breaking with the formal principles upon which music had thus far been based. Carl Czerny informs us: 'About the year 1800, when Beethoven had composed Opus 28 he said to his intimate friend, Krumpholz: "I am far from satisfied with my past works: from today on I shall take a new way." Shortly after this appeared his three sonatas Opus 31, in which one may see that he had partially carried out his resolve.'[4] However, the 'Eroica' Symphony Op. 55, composed largely in 1803, marked his irrevocable commitment to his 'new way', incorporating music of unprecedented spaciousness, breadth, power and expressive force. Compensating for his deafness through his art,[5] Beethoven systematically exploited his 'new way' in other instrumental genres, producing works of consistent quality such as the Triple Concerto Op. 56 (1803–4), the 'Appassionata' Op. 57, the G major Piano Concerto Op. 58 (1805–6), the three 'Rasumovsky' Quartets Op. 59 (1805–6) and the Fourth Symphony Op. 60 (1806). During the latter part of this same period, Beethoven composed the first and second versions of *Fidelio*, was working on his Fifth Symphony, and completed his Violin Concerto Op. 61. His new approach also manifests itself in the development of two contrasting melodic tendencies, which are particularly evident in his Violin Concerto.[6] Broad, arching, more fluid melodic lines moving at a leisurely pace appear in many of the expansive allegros, resulting in a new and individual lyricism; and particular emphasis is placed upon the smaller units, especially the motive.

Beethoven as violinist

It was by his extraordinary prowess at the piano that Beethoven initially made his way in Vienna. His technical brilliance, powerful execution and uncanny ability to improvise was constantly admired by influential members of the nobility such as Prince Lichnowsky and Baron van Swieten and he also gained the acclaim of the general public for his performances in Viennese concert venues. Although he had devoted and generous patrons, he was no servant. He enjoyed the friendship and professional support of Prince Joseph Lobkowitz, Count Andreas Rasumovsky, and his young pupil the Archduke Rudolph, and he engaged in several improvisation contests against other pianists, notably Abbé Gelinek (1758–1825) and Daniel Steibelt (1765–1823).[7]

2

Beethoven's abilities as a violinist, however, are not well documented and his knowledge of the instrument, though based on actual playing experience, bears no comparison with his creative affinity for the piano. The limited available evidence suggests that he was a comparatively mediocre player. Thayer reports that Beethoven's father Johann 'gave Ludwig instruction upon the pianoforte and violin in his earliest childhood'.[8] As a boy of nine, Ludwig is believed to have received violin and viola tuition from the young court violinist Franz Georg Rovantini, a distant member of the Beethoven family, but Rovantini's sudden death in September, 1781, seems to have brought a premature end to the youth's systematic violin instruction. Nevertheless, Beethoven was sufficiently competent a string player to participate as a violist in performances of the Electoral Court Orchestra in Bonn, gaining invaluable orchestral experience and an extensive acquaintance with operatic music.

With his friend Stephan von Breuning, Beethoven received some violin instruction from Franz Ries (1755–1838), and, after moving to Vienna, from Wenzel Krumpholz (c1750–1817) and Ignaz Schuppanzigh (1776–1830),[9] but evidently made little progress. His attempts at playing the violin part of his own violin sonatas with his pupil Ferdinand Ries resulted, according to Ries, in 'really dreadful music...because in his enthusiasm he did not hear when he began a passage with wrong fingering.'[10] Gerhard von Breuning confirms such doubts about Beethoven's violinistic skills: 'What my father [Stephan von Breuning] did say repeatedly, and he played the violin correctly all his life and was a judge of violinists, was that as a youngster, Ludwig soon became a tremendous pianist but he never had any particular purity of tone on the fiddle nor any outstanding ability on it; he was always likely to play out of tune even before his hearing was affected; thereafter, of course, his playing was increasingly out of tune until deafness made him give it up completely.'[11] Nevertheless, Beethoven was perfectly capable of making precise technical demands on players; in 1825 Sir George Smart witnessed how, during a rehearsal of the String Quartet Op. 132, 'A staccato passage not being expressed to the satisfaction of his eye, for alas, he could not hear, he [Beethoven] seized Holz's violin and played the passage a quarter of a tone too flat.'[12]

3

Apprenticeship

Beethoven seems to have served an apprenticeship for whatever medium he was writing. An early Violin Concerto fragment (WoO5), the two Romances Op. 50 in F (c1798) and Op. 40 in G (c1801–2) and the 'Kreutzer' sonata Op. 47 (1802–03), 'written in a concertante style, rather like a concerto',[13] served as preparation for his Violin Concerto, while the Triple Concerto was preceded by extensive sketches for an earlier Concertante in D.

The autograph manuscript of Beethoven's early Violin Concerto in C, dedicated to Gerhard von Breuning, is preserved in the library of the Gesellschaft der Musikfreunde, Vienna (cat. no. IX-6820). Dating from Beethoven's last years in Bonn (1790–2), its score comprises only 259 bars of an Allegro con brio first movement in 4/4 time for soloist, flute, two oboes, two bassoons, two horns and strings (including *divisi* violas).[14] The surviving fragment includes two orchestral ritornellos, the first solo and the beginning of the second solo bringing the development, the last surviving page introducing a new transition motive. As Basil Deane observes: 'the first part of the movement shows Beethoven intent on reconciling symphonic development with traditional concerto form. The opening tutti, nearly 100 bars long, contains strong contrasts of material, abrupt modulation in the transition, and a distinct second group in the dominant key, and concludes with a fully orchestrated statement of the opening fanfare in the home key.' This tendency of the opening tutti to assume a full symphonic life before the introduction of the soloist, evident, of course, in many of Mozart's late piano concertos (e.g. K.491), was mirrored also in Beethoven's Violin Concerto; and Deane rightly draws parallels between the solo writing in the two works, that of the fragment foreshadowing Op. 61 'in its lyrical use of the upper compass, and its declamatory power in the semiquaver figuration.'[15]

Much scholarly debate has focused on whether the fragment, which bears the title 'Concerto', is an unfinished fair copy or draft in score; whether it is the only surviving portion of a complete movement; or, in the latter event, whether that movement formed part of a full-length concerted work. Willy Hess considers it a fair copy and suggests that the first movement, at least, once existed in complete form.[16] However, although he admits that this is a relatively 'clean' manuscript for

4

Beethoven, Wilfried Fischer believes that 'several far-reaching corrections, especially in the solo part' suggest a draft rather than a fair copy. He explains: 'Hess's hypothesis that part of the autograph is lost depends less upon its written presentation than upon the fact that the MS breaks off at the end of a verso side and not at the end of a recto with a blank verso nor yet in the middle of a page. Moreover, all parts, including all rests, are written out in full right up to the last surviving bar (bar 259), so that it can in fact be assumed that the autograph originally contained further pages which are now missing.' Nevertheless, the confident handling of the surviving material and the fact that sketches exist from 1792/3 for a piano cadenza in G, based on the thematic material of this movement, lend further support to Hess's view.[17] Furthermore, as Basil Deane points out, it is possible that one or both of Beethoven's Romances for violin and orchestra may have been intended originally as a slow movement for this concerto:

> They are scored for the same orchestral forces...their tonalities are closely related to C major; their date of composition may be in advance of that of publication (1802) by several years, and there is nothing in the style or scale of either piece that would not accord with the concerto fragment. The writing shows the same awareness of the nature of the instrument; the emphasis is again on the upper register, but the composer is alive to the richness of the lower compass, used sparingly with telling effect.[18]

When Beethoven's manuscript for the fragment came to light (c1870), Josef Hellmesberger Sen. completed the movement, publishing it, with cadenza, in an orchestration for flute, two oboes, two bassoons, two horns, two trumpets, timpani and strings. Hellmesberger's reconstruction failed to arouse much enthusiasm, doubtless because he added trumpets and timpani to the original orchestration and treated the work in a somewhat inflated manner and style. The Spanish violinist Juan Manén brought the fragment back into the public eye in 1933, when he performed his own completion of the work in Barcelona. Published some ten years later,[19] his version has been criticised for its infidelity to the text and instrumentation of Beethoven's original.[20] August Wilhelmj's completion of the movement has also suffered criticism, particularly for the content of its recapitulation, which, according to Tovey, 'is entirely wrong. He does not know what ought to be recapitulated in a classical concerto, and he does not know how Beethoven handled such things.'[21] Not until Willy Hess's edition of 1961 was a reliable, scholarly version of this fragment published. This, in turn, inspired Wilfried Fischer's 'practical edition'; refraining entirely from interfering with the surviving musical text and instrumentation, this reconstruction comprises an additional 140 bars, 116 of which are taken from the exposition, either literally or with minor modifications such as the expected transposition of the second theme into the tonic in the recapitulation.[22]

Apart from its predominant lyrical qualities, Beethoven's Triple Concerto has little bearing on his Violin Concerto, the melodic material of its long first movement suffering from a surprising lack of development. The pair of Romances Opp. 40 and 50, however, retain many of the characteristics of the typical slow movement of French violin concertos of the 1770s – simplicity, lyricism, symmetrical phrase structure and, in the case of the G major Romance, duple time commencing at the half-bar; they may be viewed as significant precursors of the slow movement of Op. 61.

The violin and bow in the early nineteenth century

By the early nineteenth century the violin and bow had each achieved essentially their modern form. Although most of the violinists in Beethoven's circle appear to have been fully conversant both with the modifications made to the instrument and with the potentialities of the relatively new Tourte-model bow, evidence suggests that Franz Clement, who premiered Beethoven's Violin Concerto, was somewhat conservative and old-fashioned in his ways and did not take full advantage of such significant organological developments, particularly with regard to matters of bowing.

The design and construction of most of the violins made before *c*1800 were modified in the interests of increased tonal volume and brilliance, effected chiefly by subjecting the instrument to greater tensions through the use of a thinner, higher bridge and an increased playing length of string.[23] The raising of the bridge necessitated corresponding adjustments to the elevation of the neck and fingerboard, enabling the latter to follow more closely the angle of the strings and thereby allow clarity of finger stopping. A thinner, longer neck was employed, tilted back at an angle and mortised (rather than nailed) into the block for additional strength. The fingerboard was narrowed at the peg-box end and broadened somewhat towards the bridge, adopting a more markedly curved outline to match the modifications to the bridge. It was also lengthened, thus affording the violinist greater facility in the higher positions. To reinforce the instrument against the increased pressure (through the bridge) exerted on the belly, a longer, thicker bass bar was introduced, while the more substantial soundpost also played a significant part in realising the late-eighteenth-century sound ideal.

These modifications in violin construction were implemented gradually between c1760 and c1830. French makers appear to have been in the vanguard of change,[24] but it seems likely that the instruments of most, if not all, of the violinists in Beethoven's circle in the early nineteenth century would have been converted to comply with contemporary musical ideals and requirements. The consistently high tessitura of the solo part of Beethoven's Violin Concerto suggests that he was fully aware of these adjustments to the neck fitting and fingerboard and was keen to take advantage of the increased technical facility they offered in the higher positions. The fact that the quartet of string instruments presented to Beethoven in 1800 by Prince Lichnowsky has been modernised may also hold some significance in this respect, but it is not known when these alterations were carried out.

Neither the chin rest, invented c1820, nor the shoulder pad, first mentioned in Baillot's treatise of 1835,[25] would have been part of the violinist's tools-in-trade at this time. Furthermore, apart from the silver- or copper-wound gut g, violin strings would generally have been of pure gut, and their thicknesses would have varied considerably according to performers' tastes and tonal requirements.[26] Despite the increased reverence towards the more brilliant overspun d' strings and the well-publicised disadvantages of gut strings – notably the need to keep them moist, their tendency to unravel, their sensitivity to variation in atmospheric temperature, and the common incidence of knots and other imperfections[27] – the combination of plain gut e'' and a', high-twist d' and a g with copper, silver-plated copper or silver round wire close-wound on a gut core was the norm throughout the nineteenth century.

The form, dimensions, weight, materials and general construction of the violin bow were also in a state of flux during Beethoven's early career.[28] They were standardised in the 1780s by François Tourte (1747–1835), whose design gradually displaced earlier models and became the virtual blueprint for subsequent makers. Tourte eventually concluded that pernambuco wood (*Caesalpinia echinata*) best satisfied those requirements of lightness, strength and elasticity demanded by violinists of his day. He determined the ideal length of the violin bow-stick to be between 74cm and 75cm and the optimum overall weight as about 56–60g. Owing to the pronounced concave curvature of his bow-stick, Tourte opted for a hatchet-like design for the head, facing it with a protective plate (generally of ivory) and making it higher (and heavier) than before in order to prevent the hair from touching the stick when pressure was applied at the tip. He redressed the balance by adding the ferrule and metal (or tortoiseshell) inlay to the frog, back-plates and screw-button.

The amount of hair employed in the stringing of bows was also increased. To counteract its irregular bunching, Tourte widened the ribbon of hair to measure about 10mm at the nut and about 8mm at the point[29] and kept it uniformly flat and even by securing it at the frog with a ferrule, believed to have been invented by Louis Tourte (père). A wooden wedge was positioned between the hair and the bevelled portion of the frog so that the hair was pressed against the ferrule and the latter prevented from sliding off. A mother-of-pearl slide (*recouvrement*) was also fitted into a swallow-tail groove in the frog in order to conceal the hair-fastening and enhance the bow's appearance. The metal heel-plate used to strengthen the back of the frog is also believed to have been added by makers during the last decade of the eighteenth century, François Tourte being one of the first to introduce it with some consistency.

Beethoven was evidently alert to these developments in bow con-struction, his knowledge possibly deriving from Rodolphe Kreutzer, whom he had met in Vienna in 1798 and with whom he remained in cor-respondence for some years.[30] Indeed, he and Wenzel Krumpholz, his violin teacher and friend, maintained a keen interest in the works of Viotti and his circle and he is known seriously to have contemplated moving to Paris at this time.[31] Krumpholz's own awareness of the new Parisian style of violin playing is demonstrated in his *Abendunterhaltung*, a collection of violin pieces written with 'a good understanding of the instrument' and apparently with a Parisian audience in mind.[32]

The Tourte-model bow could produce a stronger tone than its predecessors and was especially well suited to the predominant cantabile style. In composing his concerto, Beethoven would doubtless have been mindful of its potential for smooth bow changes with the minimum differentiation, where required, between slurred and separate bowing. A normal straight bow stroke with the index-finger pressure and bow speed constant produced an even tone throughout its length, because the shape and flexibility of the stick allowed even finger-pressure distribution. Variation of this pressure, bow speed, contact point, type of stroke and other technical considerations provided the expressive range so important to contemporary aesthetic ideals.

The shape and consequent inferior strength of most pre-Tourte bows result in the hair being capable of considerably less tension than that of Tourte models. Thus they yield rather more when brought into contact with the strings and produce, in Leopold Mozart's words, 'a small, even if barely audible, softness at the beginning of the stroke'.[33] A similar 'softness' at the end of each stroke explains their natural articulation. The concave stick of Tourte's bows, on the other hand, yields very little on contact with the string, thereby affording a more or less immediate attack. Furthermore, its quicker take-up of hair, greater strength (particularly at the point) and resiliency and its broader ribbon of hair also contributed to widening the vocabulary of bow strokes to include true *sforzando* effects and various accented and 'springing' bowings. The *martelé*, the most fundamental of all modern strokes, formed the basis of other important bowings; even the *staccato*, the natural stroke of the upper half of most pre-Tourte bows, became a series of small successive *martelé* strokes with the Tourte model.

Universal approval of the Tourte bow was slow to materialise. Although Woldemar claims (1801) that the 'Viotti' (i.e. Tourte) model was exclusively used,[34] some French makers continued to make bows modelled on pre-Tourte designs well into the nineteenth century. Significantly, Vienna was probably the most conservative major European city when it came to instrumental innovations. Robert Winter points out that the Viennese 'maintained a near-fanatical loyalty to their simpler [piano] action well into the twentieth century' despite the significant developments in England and Paris during the first half of the nineteenth century. Interestingly, too, Leopold Mozart's *Versuch einer gründlichen*

9

Violinschule of 1756 was still popular in nineteenth-century reprintings in Vienna, so it is not surprising that few of the leading Viennese violinists adopted Viotti's bowing style, which stressed variety of slurring, long strokes and powerful tone.[35] A reviewer of Franz Clement's playing shortly before the premiere of Beethoven's Violin Concerto concluded: 'his is not the pithy, bold, powerful playing, the gripping, striking Adagio, the power of bow and tone which characterises the Rode and Viotti school: rather an indescribable delicacy, neatness and elegance; an extremely charming tenderness and clarity of performance'.[36] Beethoven's progressive attitude towards change therefore appears to conflict with Clement's somewhat old-fashioned approach. Add to this anomaly the extraordinary textual history and genesis of Beethoven's concerto and the likelihood that the *ad hoc* orchestra convened for its premiere comprised mixed groups of players, some with fully modernised instruments and Tourte bows and others who clung tenaciously to unaltered instruments with flat 'transition' bows, and reasons for the indifferent early reception history of the work become more comprehensible.

2

The genesis of Op. 61

It is one of the extraordinary paradoxes of the nineteenth century that its greatest violin concertos were written by pianists. Mendelssohn and Brahms, for example, sought the advice of distinguished violinists such as Ferdinand David and Joseph Joachim, while Beethoven assimilated the most important currents in late-eighteenth- and early-nineteenth-century string playing through his association with numerous eminent performers. During the latter part of his time in Bonn, he worked with the violin- and cello-playing Romberg cousins Andreas and Bernhard, and he frequently attended quartet parties at the home of Emanuel Aloys Förster. He became closely associated with Wenzel Krumpholz, Anton Wranitzky, Ignaz Schuppanzigh, Karl Amenda, Franz Clement, Joseph Mayseder and Joseph Boehm during his years in Vienna; and despite increasing deafness and his inclination to scoff at advice, the experience of hearing and working with other internationally acclaimed violinists who visited Vienna, particularly Rodolphe Kreutzer, George Polgreen Bridgetower and Pierre Baillot, undoubtedly contributed significantly towards his concept of violin playing. Thus, in addition to his own German background, the principal factors which influenced Beethoven in the composition of his Violin Concerto emanated from France and Vienna.

The French connection I – principal personalities

From his early career in Bonn, Beethoven was familiar with a wide variety of French music, ranging from the repertory of the pre-revolutionary *opéra comique* and the lyric dramas of the 1790s, which served as his models for *Fidelio*, to the concertos of the French violin school. He was a particular admirer of Luigi Cherubini (1760–1842), a dominant figure in French musical life at the turn of the century who visited Vienna in 1805 as an acknowledged master of the French operatic style.[1] Predominant among Beethoven's inspiration for his Violin Concerto was the work of the French violin school, the most significant member of which was Cherubini's friend, Giovanni Battista Viotti (1755–1824), a disciple of Pugnani and the last great representative of the Italian tradition stemming from Corelli. Viotti, who may have assisted Tourte in his development of the 'modern' bow,[2] soon gained favour in Paris as a violinist and composer after a somewhat mixed reception on his debut at the Concert Spirituel in 1782, playing one of his own concertos. Some objected to his style, which, they claimed, was designed 'more to astonish than to please';[3] however, by 1800, 'in Vienna and St. Petersburg, in London and Paris, everyone played Viotti'.[4] Nineteen of Viotti's twenty-nine violin concertos date from his years in Paris. They range from those in a cosmopolitan *galant* style to those whose character, drama and expressive potential were strengthened immeasurably by operatic influences, notably Nos. 14–19; but the products of Viotti's London sojourn (from 1792) surpass them in substance, drama, adventurousness, craftsmanship and solo exploitation and represent the Classical violin concerto style in its fully evolved form.

The principles of Viotti's performing style and his concept of the violin concerto were perpetuated and developed by, among others, Pierre Rode (1774–1830; thirteen violin concertos), Pierre Baillot (1771–1842; nine violin concertos) and Rodolphe Kreutzer (1766–1831; nineteen violin concertos), with all of whom Beethoven had personal contact at some stage of his career. Rode, Baillot and Kreutzer were appointed to the violin faculty of the Paris Conservatoire (established in 1795) and they encapsulated Viotti's manner of performance in their teaching, particularly through their *Méthode de violon* (1803) and Baillot's own, more comprehensive *L'art du violon...*(1835). The Viotti tradition became so ingrained in Paris that until 1853 (with one exception in 1845) no concertos other than his were used in the Conservatoire's violin competitions.[5] The resultant unique homogeneity of violin performance was reflected in the high standards of Parisian orchestras – particularly that of the Conservatoire, which performed Beethoven's First Symphony in 1807, the first performance of any of his orchestral works in Paris.

Kreutzer came to Vienna in 1798, accompanying the French ambassador, General Bernadotte. Beethoven, who was a frequent visitor at the French legation, may have met and heard Kreutzer there. In 1804, he remembered Kreutzer as 'a good, amiable man who during his stay here gave me much pleasure. His unaffectedness and natural manner are more to my taste than all *extérieur* or *intérieur* of most virtuosos.' Beethoven also obviously thought highly of Kreutzer's musical ability, dedicating his Violin Sonata Op. 47 to him and claiming: 'Since the sonata is written for a first-rate player, the dedication is all the more fitting.'[6] Such respect was evidently not mutual, for Kreutzer neither acknowledged the dedication nor performed the sonata in public – according to Berlioz, he found the work 'outrageously unintelligible'[7] – and he continued to show hostility towards Beethoven's works when François Habeneck introduced the Second Symphony to Parisian audiences.

Baillot met Beethoven and played for him in 1805. While there appears to have been little further contact between them, the Frenchman became one of the foremost champions of Beethoven's music. In 1814, he established chamber music concerts in Paris (modelled after Schuppanzigh's concerts in Vienna), which contributed decisively to the understanding of Beethoven's works in Paris, and he later became renowned for his interpretation of Beethoven's Violin Concerto.

Rode did not visit Vienna until 1812, almost six years after the Violin Concerto's premiere. His playing was apparently already on the decline by that time, Spohr for one missing 'his former boldness in conquering great difficulties.'[8] Beethoven completed the tenth and last of his violin sonatas (Op. 96) for Rode and Archduke Rudolph, commenting of the finale: 'in view of Rode's playing I have had to give more thought to the composition of this movement. In our Finales we like to have fairly noisy passages, but R[ode] does not care for them – and so I have been rather hampered.'[9] It would appear that Beethoven miscalculated somewhat, because a contemporary review of the performance reports that the piano part (played by the Archduke) was performed 'with more understanding of the work and with more soul' than the violin part. 'Mr. Rode's greatness does not seem to lie in this type of music but in the performance of the concerto.'[10] This statement might easily have been extended to include the composition of concertos, as Rode's essays in the genre proved almost as influential as Viotti's in the conception of Beethoven's single masterpiece for the violin.

The French connection II – general style, form and character

The profound influence of French 'revolutionary' music on Beethoven's style is reflected principally in his cultivation of motivic relationships, his handling of instrumental structures, and in the inspiration he derived from its general character and sonorities. Particularly significant was its overall tone of seriousness and grandeur, its militaristic quality reflective of the nationalistic revolutionary attitude; its emphasis on the voice and vocal melody; and its penchant for massive sonorities.[11] While none of these elements is unique to French music, they were generally combined in such a way as to create a national stamp, especially the manner in which melody and instrumentation were used to form grandiose and militaristic characteristics.

The military quality of much French music of the late eighteenth and early nineteenth centuries actually predates the Revolution. Alfred Einstein traced it back at least to the concertos of Viotti, which began to appear in print in the 1780s and were extremely popular throughout Europe. Referring to the first movements, he defined it as 'an idealised quick march, brisk four in a bar, with a decisive beginning, pushing boldly on, often brusque in manner; dotted quavers on the up-beats and a constantly pulsing rhythm', and pointed out that it is 'martial but not a march'.[12] Schering associated this military element in the French violin concerto with the *mood* of the Revolution and linked the genre with contemporary operatic trends: 'Attuned to brilliance and splendour, magnificence and dignity, its character reveals itself at the outset in the pompous march ritornels...symbols of a partly heroic, partly lowly *soldatesque*, mentality...The French Violin Concerto is a product of the mood of the Revolution, a blood brother of the youthful operas of Cherubini, Méhul, representing the best qualities of the French nation.'[13] This affinity between the French concerto and French 'revolutionary' opera is given greater credence by taking into account Kreutzer's success as an opera composer and the deep involvement of Viotti, Rode and Baillot in operatic activities.

Kreutzer arguably exploited the military-style concerto first movement the most, Viotti's style often tending rather towards lyricism, expression and sonority. Nevertheless, many of Viotti's Parisian concertos (Nos. 1–19) incorporate an assertive march quality; and despite the

14

military character of some of Mozart's concerto first movements, notably the violin concerto K.218 and the piano concertos K.453 and K.459, Einstein seems justified in claiming that 'It was from Viotti, and presumably not from Mozart, that Beethoven derived the idea of a "military" first movement for all his concertos.'[14]

Beethoven was undoubtedly attracted to the French aesthetic for both technical and spiritual reasons. Following generally the established three-movement pattern, the concertos of Viotti (and, indeed, Mozart) were the logical models for his works in the genre and their heroic and military content was entirely compatible with Beethoven's own musical personality. The first movement of the French violin concerto was usually divided into four orchestral ritornellos and three solos. A march-like opening was traditional but not obligatory; some concertos begin lyrically while others have the impassioned sweep and agitation of the contemporary operatic overture. The long-delayed entrance of the soloist was treated with some brilliance and was usually based on new thematic material, although occasionally the first orchestral theme was used. The second solo, generally involving contrast of mode and an intensification of expression and brilliance, was customarily a free fantasia and only rarely included true 'development' of material. The last solo normally incorporated a shortened recapitulation and a cadenza within the orchestral coda.

Of Beethoven's seven completed concertos, the Triple Concerto, a symphonie concertante in all but name, approximates most closely to the French concept. However, the Fifth Piano Concerto ('Emperor') has the most pronounced military character, 'perhaps a reflection of the war-torn year 1809, during which Beethoven also wrote two marches for military band'.[15] The first movements of the First and Second Piano Concertos are also in martial style, and while the later concertos seem less dependent upon Classical models, especially No. 3, all retain a military element. The Violin Concerto's drum motif imparts a martial character to an otherwise substantially lyrical piece, and even the Third and Fourth Piano Concertos have their share of sublimated march music, notably in the second subject of the first movement (1/29–32) and in the finale of No. 4 (3/1–10), in the drum-like (dominant–tonic) motif (which returns in the coda) incorporated in the opening theme of No. 3 (1/3–4), and in the modified orchestration of the same theme on its reappearance in the major mode (first in E♭, played by clarinets and horns (1/220–3), then in C by horns and trumpets (1/397–400). From the Third Piano Concerto onwards, however, Beethoven broadens the scope of the first movement, expanding it to symphonic proportions, combining thematic development with the free fantasia element of the French, and achieving greater concentration and economy of thematic material, which is shared by orchestra and soloist.

The central slow movements of French concertos of the period are usually *romances*, incorporating themes that recall popular song. Viotti and his disciples normally kept these movements fairly brief and unadorned – one solo framed by two brief orchestral ritornellos, with embellishments normally added by the soloist. Few of Beethoven's concerto slow movements have much in common with this genre, but, as Chapter 6 will reveal, the Violin Concerto may be considered a notable exception, which also draws inspiration from Viotti's experiments with the chaconne in his Seventh and Twenty-third Violin Concertos and demonstrates the remarkable care with which Beethoven works melodic elaborations into his text. Occasionally, the second movement of French concertos led without break into the finale, a principle that Beethoven also adopted in some of his concertos, notably his Violin and Triple Concertos and the Fourth and Fifth Piano Concertos.

French finales are normally brilliant, witty rondeaux, the form sometimes accommodating a variety of genre pieces, foreign tunes or dance rhythms; for example, the rondeau of Viotti's Thirteenth Violin Concerto is a lively polonaise. Beethoven acknowledged this trend briefly in the First Piano Concerto's gypsy-like interlude (3/191–273), in the Triple Concerto's 'Rondo alla polacca', and in the Violin Concerto's chasse-like principal theme (3/1–8) and striking G minor episode featuring the bassoon (3/126–58).

The French connection III – violin idiom

Beethoven's familiarity with the compositions and playing styles of leading figures of the French violin school led to his transforming some of their idiomatic features from simple bravura to embellishments of profound musical ideas. Boris Schwarz cites several similarities between

2.1 Viotti: Violin Concerto No. 22 in A minor (2nd movement)

Beethoven's violin writing in Op. 61 and that of his French models, these similarities extending to the shape and character of some of the thematic material as well as to the exploitation of the instrument's technical resources.[16] Bars 60–8 of Beethoven's Larghetto, for example, have a close affinity with a passage from the Adagio of Viotti's Concerto No. 22 (Ex. 2.1) 'not only in the melodic line and supporting harmonies but in the whole manner in which the phrase is placed within the context of the movement'. Many of the broken octave figurations exploited by Beethoven in the outer movements of his Violin Concerto could well have been derived directly from the scores of Viotti and Kreutzer (Exx. 2.2–2.4); similarly, the famous passage in sixths in Beethoven's finale (3/68–73 and 243–8) finds a close precedent in the first movement of Viotti's Fifth Violin Concerto (Ex. 2.5). Furthermore, Schwarz shows how Viotti's characteristic elaboration of a melodic line in triplets is mirrored in Beethoven's opening movement (Ex. 2. 6), and he is equally persuasive in his suggestion that Beethoven drew inspiration also from Kreutzer's distinctive approach to such melodic embellishment (Exx. 2.7 and 2.8). Add to these examples the similarities between Beethoven's treatment of his timpani motif in the first movement and Viotti's use of a repeated-note motif in the parallel movement of his

2.2 Viotti: Violin Concerto No. 1 in C major (1st movement)

2.3 Kreutzer: Violin Concerto No. 6 in E minor (1st movement)

2.4 Viotti: Violin Concertos Nos. 1 in C major and 6 in E major (3rd movements)

2.5 Viotti: Violin Concerto No. 5 in C major (1st movement)

Concerto No. 26; the common linking of the second and third movements of Viotti's concertos and its parallels with Beethoven; the precedents in Viotti's finales (e.g. Nos. 22, 27, 28 and 29) for the type of accompanied cadenza included in the first movement of Beethoven's piano adaptation, Op. 61a; and the relation of Beethoven's rondo

2.6 Viotti: Violin Concerto No. 1 in C major (1st movement)

2.7 Kreutzer: Violin Concertos Nos. 4 in C major and 13 in D major (1st movements)

2.8 Kreutzer: Violin Concerto No. 16 in E minor (1st movement)

themes to those of Viotti's Sixth Concerto, and it is evident that one may legitimately regard much of Beethoven's Violin Concerto as an individual and advanced interpretation of the French school's, and especially Viotti's, conception.

Though based on actual playing experience, Beethoven's violin writing bears no comparison with his creative affinity for the piano and sometimes seems to have been derived from the keyboard. He refrained almost entirely from emulating the French school's exploitation of double stopping and sonorous sul G string effects (except for the first movement's coda statement of the lyrical second theme at b. 511 and the soloist's statement of the finale's principal theme at, for example, bb. 1–9). Instead, he shows a distinct preference for the higher registers of the E string and makes fairly modest technical demands of the solo violinist, emphasising the lyrical qualities of the instrument and shifting the dramatic accents and gestures into the orchestra.

Austrian influences

Beethoven's use of the concerto orchestra owes its inspiration largely to works of Austrian composers such as Leopold Hofmann, Carl Ditters von Dittersdorf and most especially Mozart. The latter absorbed the influence of J. C. Bach as well as 'formal unity from Vienna, thematic sophistication from Mannheim, and rhythmic continuity from Italy'.[17] His five violin concertos, all early works (1775), testify to his experimentation and ripening craftsmanship; but his achievement in fusing concertante and symphonic elements, accomplished principally through his piano concertos, had far-reaching consequences in the history of the genre, resulting in a new kind of integration between soloist and orchestra which Beethoven exploited to the full. However, Mozart's influence notwithstanding, Beethoven's most direct Austrian inspiration probably emanated from the concertos and performing style of Franz Clement, who premiered Beethoven's violin concerto and undoubtedly influenced its style and content.

Franz Clement – I: performing style

Clement was a child prodigy on the violin, a fine pianist and orchestral conductor. He was very much in the centre of Viennese musical activity at the beginning of the nineteenth century and became an esteemed friend of Beethoven and a champion of his works, introducing several of them to a somewhat reluctant Viennese public. Proclaimed 'the most artistic violinist in Vienna',[18] Clement's playing is reported to have been graceful and lyrical rather than vigorous, with a comparatively small yet expressive tone, and an assured left-hand technique, especially in the higher registers of the instrument. Such an elegant style was somewhat outmoded in the wake of the Viotti school, but proved especially influential in the genesis of Beethoven's concerto, whose 'true greatness', according to Ysaÿe, 'lies, not in the technique, but in the *cantilena*'.[19]

Clement began playing the violin at the early age of four, receiving early instruction from his father, Joseph, and later from Kurzweil, the concertmaster of Prince Grassalkovich. His first significant public concert in Vienna on 11 April 1788 was followed by two further acclaimed appearances there in 1789. Such success urged Franz's father to escort him on a three-year tour, taking in South Germany and Belgium and culminating in practically a two-year sojourn in England, where Franz appeared twice before the King at Windsor and participated fully in the musical life of the capital. He also associated with the likes of Haydn and Salomon, and, using London as his base, made shorter concert tours to various provincial centres. He returned to Vienna via Amsterdam and various other Dutch cultural centres, Frankfurt and Prague.

On his return to Vienna, he became involved in a kind of violin contest with Viotti, was invited to play for the Emperor and embarked on an acrobatic 'showbiz' manner of performance, participating in a concert in which a concerto 'on the reversed violin, solely on the G-string' was the special attraction.[20] He also obtained an appointment in the National Theater as soloist and assistant to the conductor, Süssmayr, joined the Emperor's chamber-music ensemble, became director (with Gebler) of the orchestra (and later 'music director') in the Theater an der Wien, and was a focal point of the flourishing Viennese concert life. His concert tour to Russia in 1811 was foreshortened by his arrest and imprisonment, on suspicion of being a spy; meanwhile, Casimir von Blumenthal had assumed his place in Vienna, forcing Clement to seek employment elsewhere. On Spohr's recommendation, Weber selected him as conductor of the orchestra and deputy director of the Prague opera.

Life turned sour again for Clement when Weber was succeeded by Triebensee at Prague. He soon resigned, returning to Vienna (1817) as music director at the Theater an der Wien. His popularity in the Austrian capital was in rapid decline, however, not least with Beethoven, who rejected him as concertmaster for a performance of the Ninth Symphony (1824) and commented, 'He has lost a great deal, and seems too old to be entertaining with his capers on the fiddle.'[21] Little is known of his later musical life, other than that he spent most of it as an itinerant musician, largely touring in South Germany, and generally fell foul of public criticism on account of his inability to move with the times. He eventually died in poverty in Vienna on 3 November 1842.

Seven years before Clement's death, his close friend Ignaz von

Seyfried paid tribute to his qualities as a youthful violinist, but criticised him for failing to make the best use of his talent.[22] Almost alone of the celebrated players of his generation, Clement neglected to cultivate the acclaimed performing qualities of the ascendant Viotti school. Contemporary descriptions of his performances generally include reference to the 'customary elegance and grace' of his playing, but neither extreme virtuosity nor tonal power appears to have been among his strengths.[23] Clement's stubborn adherence to his own style proved to be his downfall. After praising his technical mastery, one critic commented that 'his short bowstroke and overwhelming mannerisms, which certainly do not allow him to achieve an expressive cantabile, will always exclude him from the ranks of the *great* violinists'; and a review of one of his performances of Beethoven's Violin Concerto in Vienna in 1833 sums up contemporary opinion of his talent: 'He is what he was; but not what he might have been.'[24]

Beethoven first heard Clement in 1794 when the violinist was already a popular figure in Viennese concert life and widely acclaimed as a solo performer. He was clearly enamoured then with Clement's playing, for he wrote in Clement's *Stammbuch*, an album dedicated to 'the eternal remembrance of his tours':

Dear Clement:

Go forth on the way in which you hitherto have travelled so beautifully, so magnificently. Nature and art vie with each other in making you a great artist. Follow both and, never fear, you will reach the great – the greatest – goal possible to an artist here on earth.

All wishes for your happiness, dear youth; and return soon, that I may again hear your dear, magnificent playing.

> Entirely your friend,
> L. v. Beethoven
> In the service of His
> Serene Highness the
> Elector of Cologne

Vienna, 1794[25]

Although rare, there are sufficient examples in Beethoven's oeuvre to suggest that he occasionally tailored music specifically to suit particular performers and their playing styles. The Wind Octet Op. 103 (and its companion Rondo, WoO25), for example, was probably written for a group of musicians at the Electoral Court in Bonn, while the Trio for piano, flute and bassoon (WoO37) was written in Bonn for Count von Westerholt and two of his children.[26] The Op. 12 Violin Sonatas of 1799 were probably influenced by Kreutzer's playing, which Beethoven greatly admired, while the Violin Sonata Op. 96 took account of Rode's performing style. Furthermore, the 'Hammerklavier' Sonata was written for Archduke Rudolph and the Violin Concerto specifically for Clement.

The relationship between Beethoven and Clement seems to have been such that Clement would certainly have considered himself free to suggest major alterations to Beethoven's violin writing. However, although we may never know with certainty that Beethoven himself sanctioned every note of the final printed version of the solo part, it seems highly unlikely that he would have entrusted the formulation of that version to anyone else. It may be, of course, that Clement and Beethoven were at loggerheads over the appropriateness of certain passagework, which might explain the disorderly nature of the manuscript and the various last-minute panics before the premiere; and it would be wrong to underestimate the interaction between the composer's initial thoughts, the special requirements of the instrument and Clement's artistic and technical values.

Beethoven's autograph, with its crossings-out and emendations, confirms the impression that the concerto was composed in some haste and completed only just in time for its premiere, but doubts have been raised regarding the veracity of Thayer's statement that Clement was obliged to play the solo part virtually at sight, without any previous rehearsal.[27] However, the likelihood that Clement cooperated with Beethoven closely on the end product – the similarities between Beethoven's work and Clement's D major Violin Concerto, outlined in the next section, arguably substantiate this theory – and the fact that Clement was celebrated among his contemporaries for his exceptional memory add some credibility to Thayer's statement. Spohr, for example, relates that Clement, after hearing two rehearsals and one performance of his oratorio *The Last Judgement*, performed whole sections of it from memory without having seen the score.[28] Similarly, he is reputed to have made a piano score of Haydn's *Creation* with only the libretto to guide him, after having heard the work several times. It is said that Haydn thought enough of Clement's piano reduction to adopt it for publication. Schindler describes a similar experience with Cherubini's opera *Faniska* in 1806; the Parisian opera composer declared that he had never encountered anyone with a memory for music that was even comparable to Clement's.[29]

Franz Clement – II: Violin Concerto in D major

Although Beethoven's Violin Concerto had a number of elements in common with the genre as cultivated by Viotti and the French violin school, it also drew on distinctive Viennese characteristics, as perpetuated in Clement's styles of performance and composition. To judge from the appearance of the manuscript, Beethoven did not find the composition of the violin part easy, and, despite the lack of firm evidence, it has commonly been supposed that many of the revisions contained therein may have been influenced by Clement. Evidence suggests, however, that Clement's influence over Beethoven extends further than has previously been documented. Although an old Viennese tradition that Clement himself provided the theme for the finale of Beethoven's Concerto cannot be substantiated,[30] it is apparent that Clement's own Violin Concerto in D major, premiered by its composer on 7 April 1805, some twenty months before the first performance of Beethoven's work, has elements in common with the later work such that Beethoven may well have used it as a model.[31]

Significantly, Beethoven participated in the same concert, directing his 'Eroica' Symphony. Having shown little appreciation of the 'Eroica', one reviewer remarked that the first and last movements of Clement's concerto were splendidly composed and beautifully scored, but that the slow movement was pleasant rather than profound.[32] This concerto is among the small number of Clement's works to have been published (Vienna, *c*1806); it may confidently be identified as the concerto he played in April 1805, for apart from mentioning its key, the reviewer remarked that the slow movement was in the style of the *Romanze* in Mozart's D minor Piano Concerto K.466. Such a parallel is perfectly appropriate in respect of Clement's slow movement, with its more animated third episode (G minor).

2.9 Clement: Violin Concerto in D major (1st movement)

The violin concertos of Clement and Beethoven have more in
common than their home key. They share similar orchestral forces –
flute, two oboes, two clarinets, two bassoons, two horns, two trumpets,
timpani, violin soloist and strings – although these are differently
deployed, especially in the slow central movements. Beethoven omits the
flute, oboes, trumpets and timpani from his Larghetto, while Clement
reserves the clarinets exclusively for his Adagio, scored for flute, clarinets, bassoons, horns, soloist and strings. Furthermore, the individual
movements share some similarities of outline, Clement's 404-bar
opening Allegro maestoso almost matching Beethoven's first movement
for length (535 bars), if not for symphonic architecture or musical
imagination and ingenuity, and his first solo entry following an orchestral exposition of 106 bars (18 bars longer than Beethoven's) in which
there is a significant martial element (Ex. 2.9). Clement also incorporates
some major/minor contrast of thematic material, notably with the first
movement's second theme (compare bb. 35ff. with bb. 340ff.); such a
ploy is used even more by Beethoven, especially with his equivalent thematic material (1/43–63). Although it is not surprising that the finales of
both concertos are rondo designs in 6/8 metre, the similarity of their

25

2.10 Clement: Violin Concerto in D major (1st movement)

beginnings is noteworthy, the soloist in both cases introducing the principal theme above a fairly sparse string accompaniment before it is taken up by the full orchestra.

Clement's central rondo Adagio (B♭ major) is essentially an instrumental *romance*, though not so labelled, in the more usual 3/4 metre. After a stark four-bar introduction, the soloist provides a link to the main rondo idea, a simple, unadorned sixteen-bar melody which reappears in varied form after each of the movement's three episodes, whether the modification be through elaboration, harmony, texture or orchestration. The third and most substantial episode takes the form of a *più moto* section in G minor, in which the soloist decorates in triplet semiquavers the melody played by the flute. Although the movement has some elements in common with Beethoven's Larghetto, notably its derivation from the *romance* and its exploitation of variation treatment for each reprise of the main rondo theme, the similarities between the two movements are not especially striking; furthermore, Clement's Adagio does not lead straight into the finale.

Although Clement's concerto is more virtuosic than Beethoven's, the solo parts of the two works have various figurations and passagework in common. The triplet figuration in octaves of Clement's first movement (Ex. 2.10) finds a close parallel in Beethoven's solo elaboration of the second theme in its minor-mode version from 1/152. An arpeggio/scale triplet figure and orchestral punctuation in the same movement of Clement's work (Ex. 2.11, with a parallel at bb. 329–32) find their match late in Beethoven's Allegro (1/469–73); and the end of Clement's first solo section (Ex. 2.12, bb. 192–200) strikes two close parallels with Beethoven's figuration in 1/199–205. Like several examples of broken octaves employed by members of the French violin school (see Ex. 2.2), the beginning of Clement's subsequent solo passage (Ex. 2.13) perhaps anticipates the initial solo entry in octaves of Beethoven's concerto

26

2.11 Clement: Violin Concerto in D major (1st movement)

2.12 Clement: Violin Concerto in D major (1st movement)

2.13 Clement: Violin Concerto in D major (1st movement)

2.14 Clement: Violin Concerto in D major (1st movement)

2.15 Clement: Violin Concerto in D major (1st movement)

2.16 Clement: Violin Concerto in D major (2nd movement)

(1/89), while Exx. 2.14 and 2.15 have striking parallels with 1/321–3 and 1/413–15 of Beethoven's work. Many of these melodic resemblances are so close that it is likely that Beethoven either unconsciously recollected passages from Clement's work or perhaps even made deliberate reference to them. Alternatively, as Clive Brown has suggested, Beethoven, by incorporating some of Clement's ideas, may equally well be demonstrating to his violinist friend how more tellingly he might have exploited those ideas.

The two slow movements have less in common from a thematic standpoint, but Ex. 2.16 demonstrates some similarity of contour with 2/50–1 of Beethoven's Larghetto and the arpeggio passage in the G minor episode of Clement's Adagio (Ex. 2.17) may well have inspired Beethoven in 1/315–21. The various rondo themes and related passagework have little direct resemblance, but figurations from Clement's finale would by no means seem misplaced in Beethoven's and vice versa. Finally, there is one particular trill pattern in Clement's first movement, just before the cadenza (Ex. 2.18), which spawns a twin just

2.17 Clement: Violin Concerto in D major (2nd movement)

2.18 Clement: Violin Concerto in D major (1st movement)

after the cadenza of Beethoven's finale (3/280–93), although the under-lying structural purpose and harmony of each example are quite differ-ent. Interestingly, Clement's use of the pattern is followed by a tutti *forte* outburst, which is reminiscent of Beethoven's dramatic gesture in, for example, 1/28.

Although there is much in Clement's concerto that has no close paral-lel in Beethoven's Op. 61, it must be admitted that the style of violin writing in Beethoven's concerto is very different to that of, for example, his Triple Concerto. A clear case can therefore be made for attributing this difference to Beethoven's objective of tailoring his concerto to suit the particular neat, elegant and lyrical playing style of Clement; for, while Beethoven clearly did not need Clement's concerto as a model, it seems reasonable to believe that it served as a useful point of departure for him in the achievement of his goal.

3

Reception and performance history

The premiere

Although public concert life in Beethoven's Vienna was unable to match that in the palaces of the nobility, it was nevertheless buoyant in the first decade of the nineteenth century.[1] The concerts were mostly one-off ventures held in appropriate theatres, restaurant salons or multi-purpose halls, for, unlike other major European cities such as London, Paris or Leipzig, the Austrian capital did not foster a continuing tradition of public subscription concerts until Ignaz Schuppanzigh's comparatively unambitious Augarten series. Single concerts were either charity concerts (for example, those of the Tonkünstler-Societät from 1772) or benefit concerts for the musician who organised them. It was in such a 'große musikalische Akademie' for the benefit of Franz Clement at the Schauspielhaus an der Wien on 23 December 1806 that Beethoven's Violin Concerto received its premiere. The first part of the concert also included works by Méhul, Handel and Mozart, while the second part featured works by Cherubini, Handel and Mozart and a further solo 'spot' for Clement, in which he followed some improvisations with 'a Sonata on one string played with the violin upside down'(see Fig. 3.1).

The Concerto gained a mixed reception. Some critics of the day considered it too long and lacking in continuity. Johann Nepomuk Möser, a man of considerable standing in the social life of his day, wrote:

The distinguished violinist Klement [sic] played, amongst other excellent pieces, also a violin concerto by Beethofen [sic], which on account of its originality and its many beautiful passages, was received with much approbation. Klement's well-known art and charm, his power and perfect command of the violin, which is his slave, were greeted with deafening

Figure 3.1 Poster advertising Franz Clement's benefit concert at which he
premiered Beethoven's Violin Concerto Op. 61

applause...With regard to Beethhofen's concerto, the opinion of all connoisseurs is the same; while they acknowledge that it contains some fine things, they agree that the continuity often seems to be completely disrupted, and that the endless repetitions of a few commonplace passages could easily lead to weariness. It is being said that Beethhofen ought to make better use of his admittedly great talents, and give us works like his first Symphonies in C and D, his charming Septet in E♭, the spirited Quintet in D and others of his earlier compositions, which will assure him of a permanent place among the foremost composers. It is feared, though, that if Beethhofen continues to follow his present course, it will go ill both with him and the public. The music could soon fail to please anyone not completely familiar with the rules and difficulties of the art. Burdened by a host of unconnected and piled-up ideas, and a continual tumult of different instruments which should merely create a characteristic effect at their entry, he could only leave the concert with an unpleasant sense of exhaustion. The audience in general were extremely pleased by this Concerto and by Klement's improvising.[2]

The attitude of the *Allgemeine Musikalische Zeitung* towards Beethoven's works tended to mirror that of its editor for its first twenty years, Friedrich Rochlitz: 'awed, but sceptical', generally reflecting 'neither condemnation nor outright acceptance.'[3] The issue of 7 January 1807 reports blandly: 'Admirers of Beethoven's muse will be interested to learn that this composer has written a violin concerto – his first, so far as I know – which the violinist Klement, who is popular here [in Vienna] has played at a concert given for his benefit with his customary elegance and grace.'[4] Such a brief report reflects Beethoven's standing with the editorship of this journal at that time, but his esteem increased steadily such that from 1810 onwards his significant works were given fuller coverage, regardless of the critic's opinion.[5] A performance of Beethoven's Concerto by Clement in 1807 was rather more successful, according to Beethoven's admittedly unreliable amanuensis, Anton Schindler,[6] and Clement kept the work in his repertory, performing it, for example, in Dresden (1815) and in Vienna (1833). He gained another mixed reception on this latter occasion, due more to his style of playing – contemporary reviews criticise his old-fashioned bowing style and his rough, piercing tone[7] – than to any deficiency in the work itself. Conversely, a performance of the work in Kassel (February, 1829) by the Baillot pupil Adolf Wiele (1794–c1853) was praised by one critic, who added the rider: 'Many listeners wished that he [Wiele] had chosen a different composition.'[8]

After the premiere

The concerto's cool introduction to the repertory is reflected in the dearth of documented performances in the thirty years or so following its premiere. As late as 1855, Louis Spohr, who rejected the late works of Beethoven while enthusiastically approving of early Wagner, is reported to have said to Joachim after a performance of the concerto, 'This is all very nice, but now I'd like to hear you play a *real* violin piece';[9] and a reviewer of Joachim's performance at the London Philharmonic Concerts in May, 1844, noted that Beethoven's 'concerto...has been generally regarded by violin-players as not a proper and effective development of the powers of that instrument.'[10] Indeed, the description 'ungrateful and unplayable' has many times been applied to the work, but it is, nonetheless, surprising that violinists such as Spohr, who was a great admirer of Rode and the French violin school and had written his first five violin concertos before Beethoven had completed his Op. 61, gave scant attention to its merits.

Many of Beethoven's works were misunderstood during his lifetime and suffered almost immediate neglect, most notably the Mass in D, the Ninth Symphony, and the 'late' quartets, nicknamed for some time the 'crazy' quartets by some critics. It was only long after Beethoven's death, in the early 1840s, that repeated performances of these works made Viennese audiences understand and appreciate their significance. The Violin Concerto seems to have suffered a similar fate, although Jacob Dont's preface to his edition of the work suggests that it was performed rather more frequently during Beethoven's lifetime than is usually thought:

> Several deviations from the older editions will not escape the attentive player of this edition of Beethoven's Violin Concerto. On the basis of reliable tradition Professor Jac. Dont in Vienna is in a position to write down much of the generally accepted version which differs especially in the tone-shadings. His father, first cellist in the Imperial and Royal Court Opera in Vienna in Beethoven's time, heard and accompanied the Violin Concerto, written for the then violin virtuoso Fr. Clement, *from the first*

performance on, very often, again also in Beethoven's presence. Solicitous for the education of his son, to whom he taught the violin at that time, he noted and marked very precisely the version wished for by Beethoven. What the youth learned then, the experienced teacher has now reproduced in the present edition with critical discrimination. All dynamic signs, fingerings and such like are, however, the independent contribution of the editor.[11]

Following its premiere, only a few performances of the concerto stand out during a long period of apparent neglect: by, for example, Luigi Tomasini Jun. (Berlin, 1812); Pierre Baillot (Paris, 1828); Henri Vieuxtemps (Vienna, 1834); Friedrich Barnbeck (Stuttgart, 1834); Karl Wilhelm Uhlrich (Leipzig, 1836); and Jérôme Gulomy (Leipzig, 1841). Baillot played the work under Habeneck's direction on 23 March 1828, shortly after Beethoven's death, at a Beethoven festival concert, the second concert of the inaugural season of Habeneck's Société des Concerts du Conservatoire. As at the premiere, critics gave more praise to the soloist's playing than to the content and status of the work: 'Here our aversion for concertos has not been maintained due to the disciplined and brilliant playing of this famous violinist [Baillot]. We admired the vigour, mellowness and neatness of his execution. These valuable qualities held us breathless until the end of the piece, which, we must say, was full of charm and grace.'[12] Fétis, however, was more positive. While praising Baillot's performance, he described the concerto as

> one of the most beautiful musical conceptions one can imagine. Admirable in both its structure and ideas, this piece was a continuous enchantment for the audience. Charming phrases, unexpected modulations, piquant orchestral effects, all are gathered together in this work. But to produce the full effect intended by the composer needs a virtuoso of the first class, a man who combines to the highest degree a perfect technique on the instrument, a passionate soul and the most exquisite feeling: all this can be found in Mr. Baillot.[13]

Baillot was invited to perform the concerto again on 11 May in the same season's sixth concert. Then followed years of unexplained neglect for the work by the Société until Delphin Alard performed it on 17 January 1847.[14]

The Leipzig-born pupil of Spohr, Friedrich Wilhelm Eichler, appears to have started a trend for the work's greater popularity in his native city when he performed 'the seldom played violin concerto of Beethoven' there in 1833. Eight years later, the correspondent of the *Allgemeine Musikalische Zeitung* suggests that the work was somewhat better known and expresses surprise that it was not heard even more often:

> Most interesting is the Violin Concerto in D major, the only one known from or written by Beethoven. We have heard it frequently over several years in Leipzig and always with enjoyment. In outline, it follows the customary concerto form and is so interesting as a composition, as well as so gratifying to the player as a solo piece, that we must express our astonishment that it is not chosen more often by tasteful violin virtuosos for the public domain. Moreover, the two additional cadenzas give the player splendid opportunity to shine not only as a virtuoso but also as a skilful artist. Mr. *Jérôme Gulomy*, whose acquaintance we have made for the first time in this concerto, performed it very beautifully, intelligently and tenderly and with an artistic unanimity, which is peculiar only to genuine talent and a truly educated artistic mind.[15]

The age of Joachim and Vieuxtemps

Beethoven's Violin Concerto did not make its appearance in any programme of the London Philharmonic Society until 9 April 1832, when it was performed by the Frankfurt-born violinist Eliason, who also played it several times in his native city in the early 1840s.[16] It was not very well received by London audiences. *The Athenaeum*'s reviewer was critical of Eliason's tone and execution and claimed that 'nothing short of the vigour, physical and mental, of a Baillot, or Paganini, could produce effect in this wild imaginative effusion of Beethoven.' By contrast, the *Harmonicon* reported: 'Beethoven has put forth no strength in his violin concerto; it is a *fiddling* affair, and might have been written by any third or fourth rate composer. We cannot say that the performance of this concealed any of its weakness, or rendered it at all more palatable.'[17] Twelve years later, however, London audiences witnessed one of the most significant performances of the work at the Fifth Philharmonic Society Concert (Hanover Square Rooms, May 27 1844) by the then twelve–year-old Joseph Joachim, under Mendelssohn. Performing the work also in Berlin (1852) and Düsseldorf (1853), both times under Schumann's direction, and at many other venues, Joachim was the first violinist to play the concerto so consistently that he established for it a permanent place in the violin repertory. As Eugène Ysaÿe remarked in the mid 1880s, Joachim played the work

> so well that he now seems part of it. It was he...who showed it to the world as a masterpiece. Without his ideal interpretation the work might have been lost among those compositions which are placed on one side and forgotten. He revived it, transfigured it, increased its measure. It was a consecration, a sort of Bayreuth on a reduced scale, in which tradition was perpetuated and made beautiful and strong...Joachim's interpretation was as a mirror in which the power of Beethoven was reflected.[18]

Critical opinion of the day certainly backs up Ysaÿe's enthusiasm. Mendelssohn, who, in Joachim's case, persuaded the committee of the Philharmonic Society not to enforce its regulation that prohibited the appearance of infant prodigies at its concerts, was full of admiration for Joachim's performance.[19] The critic of *The Musical World* referred to the 'almost novelty of Beethoven's violin concerto', and described Joachim's performance as

> astonishing. Not only was it astonishing as coming from a comparative child, but astonishing as a violin performance, no matter from whom proceeding. The greatest violinists hold this concerto in awe. It is, we must own, not adapted to display advantageously the powers of the instrument, though a composition of great distinction, the first movement being in Beethoven's highest manner. Young Joachim, however, attacked it with the vigour and determination of the most accomplished artist, and made every point tell. So well did he play, that we forgot how entirely unadapted for display was the violin part. No master could have read it better, no finished artist could have better rendered it. Tone, execution, and reading were alike admirable – and the two cadences [cadenzas] introduced by the young player were not only tremendous executive feats, but ingeniously composed – consisting wholly of excellent and musician-like workings of phrases and passages from the concerto. The reception of Joachim was enthusiastic, and his success the most complete and triumphant that his warmest friends could have desired.

The Morning Post carried similar ecstatic reviews, claiming that Joachim's performance of the concerto 'was altogether unprecedented, and elicited from amateurs and professors equal admiration'.

The critic of the *Allgemeine Musikalische Zeitung* wrote of a Joachim performance in Leipzig: 'Joachim...not only gave evidence of the important advance he has made in technical skill, but also showed that he has developed so far as to grasp the spiritual meaning of a work of the highest artistic importance. The manner in which he performed the difficult and inspired concerto of Beethoven precludes every doubt as to his vocation for the musical profession, and sets him far above the mere virtuosi in the ranks of the artists.'[20] His performance of the Beethoven concerto under Schumann's direction at the Düsseldorf Musikfest in May 1853 drew the following praise from Clara Schumann: 'Joachim was the crown of the evening...he celebrated a victory greater than any of us. But he played with such poetry, such perfection, with so much soul in every note – really ideal – I have never heard violin playing like it. Never before did I receive such an unforgettable impression from a virtuoso.'[21]

Henri Vieuxtemps (1820–81) became another significant champion of Beethoven's Violin Concerto. Following his acclaimed performance of the work in Vienna as a teenager in 1834, apparently at the behest of Holz and with only two weeks' preparation,[22] one critic claimed that Vieuxtemps would never give a more accurate and intelligible, clean, perfect, spirited and expressive performance of the piece in his whole life, while the conductor Eduard von Lannoy, director of the Vienna Conservatoire, praised his 'original, novel and yet classical manner' of interpretation.[23] Vieuxtemps gave another 'truly masterly' performance of this 'glorious' work in Frankfurt in 1843 and played it again in Vienna in 1854, moving Eduard Hanslick to write: 'Listening to Vieuxtemps is one of the greatest, most unqualified pleasures music has to offer. His playing is as technically infallible and masterly as it is musically noble, inspired, and compelling. I consider him the first among contemporary violinists. Some may counter with Joachim...but for one who has not heard Joachim, the existence of a greater player than Vieuxtemps is hard to imagine.'[24] Interestingly, Hanslick did hear Joachim play the concerto seven years later (1861) and compared the two violinists' performances thus:

At the close of the first movement it must have been clear to every one that this was not merely an astonishing *virtuoso*, but an eminent and striking personality. Joachim, with all his *bravura*, is so completely lost in the musical ideal, that one might almost describe him as having passed through the most brilliant *virtuosity* to perfect musicianship.

His playing is great, noble, and free...The Beethoven Concerto, especially the free, deeply emotional performance of the adagio (which almost sounded like an improvisation), proved the most decided independence of

interpretation. Under Vieuxtemps' bow the concerto sounded more brilliant and lively; Joachim's interpretation was deeper, and surpassed, with
truly ethical power, the effect which Vieuxtemps obtained by reason of his
temperament.[25]

Ysaÿe and other nineteenth-century virtuosos

Early-nineteenth-century virtuosos such as Ole Bull (1810–80) and
Niccolò Paganini (1782–1840) appear to have turned their backs on
public performance of Beethoven's Concerto. Bull was 'somewhat suspi-
cious' of Beethoven and 'was never able to interpret this composer's
music to his own satisfaction'.[26] Paganini, on the other hand, was a great
admirer of Beethoven; although there is no record of Paganini ever
having played the Beethoven Concerto in public, there is evidence of his
familiarity with it.[27] However, the Czech violinist Ferdinand Laub
(1832–75) identified himself with Beethoven's Concerto and contributed much to its dissemination as performer and teacher, gaining high
praise in Prague (7 July 1858) for one of his numerous performances.
Henryk Wieniawski (1835–80) also had great success with the work. At a
concert in the Paris Conservatoire he played it 'with the precision of a
machine, with the breadth of tone and beautiful singing quality which
make him one of the most outstanding talents'.[28] Evidence of the concerto's gradual acceptance into the violin repertory is provided by the
fact that it was included eight times in the programmes of the Société des
Concerts in Paris between April 1859 and April 1885.

When Sarasate (1844–1908) performed it in Berlin in the early 1880s,
critics compared him unfavourably with Joachim. Even Carl Flesch, an
admirer of Sarasate, admitted that 'as an interpreter of the Beethoven
Concerto, Sarasate was impossible'; and Vsevolod Cheshikhin, comparing Sarasate's and Ysaÿe's interpretations, reported that Sarasate used to
imbue the concerto 'with so much fire and power that he has accustomed
the public to an entirely different understanding of this work; at any rate',
he concludes, 'the graceful and tender treatment of Ysaÿe is very inter-
esting'.[29] By contrast, Hugo Heermann's (1844–1935) performance on
his Parisian debut in 1893 with Lamoureux gained favour with Flesch on
account of his German attitude and his faithfulness to the work.[30] Flesch
(1873–1944) was himself renowned for a similar fidelity, and Reger con-

sidered him (1912) the 'best interpreter of Beethoven's Violin Concerto', his interpretation having 'noble grandeur and inner warmth'.[31]

'The most outstanding and individual violinist I have ever heard in my life'[32] was how Flesch described Eugène Ysaÿe (1858–1931), who apparently did not tackle Beethoven's Violin Concerto until he was in his early thirties. Inspired initially by Joachim's interpretation, Ysaÿe gradually forged a very different concept of the work, emphasising its grand and noble simplicity and its lyrical, expressive qualities. His policy of valuing interpretation more highly than textual fidelity in order 'to bring music to life'[33] often invited criticism. Flesch remarked: 'in his [Ysaÿe's] hands the Beethoven concerto suffered an imaginative remodelling of the original into a personal experience, which did not leave much of the unadulterated Beethoven spirit'; and the critic of *The World*, having extolled the merits of Joachim's interpretation of the Beethoven concerto, asks: 'who can think of Beethoven, or even of music, whilst Ysaÿe is Titanically emphasising himself and his stupendous accomplishment, elbowing aside the conductor, eclipsing the little handful of an orchestra which he thinks sufficient for a concert in St. James's Hall, and all but showing Beethoven the door? The fact is, he has created himself so recently that he is not yet tired of the novelty of his own consummated self.'[34] Fourteen years later, Nikolai Kaskin reported a less indulgent, more mature approach: 'Ysaÿe seemed to lose himself in an awesome contemplation, and his playing was stamped with a majestic calm imbued with a deep and sincere feeling.'[35]

After its somewhat slow acceptance during the first half-century of its existence, Beethoven's Violin Concerto gradually gained in popularity in the latter half of the nineteenth century, thanks principally to the inspirational performances of Joachim, Vieuxtemps, Flesch and Ysaÿe. It has since entered the repertory of most violinists of the current century and has become arguably the focal work and one of the most recorded examples of its genre.

The age of recordings

Recordings provide an invaluable resource for tracing the performance history of this concerto in the twentieth century, preserving for posterity numerous violinists' interpretations of the work and revealing how performing styles have changed over the years, particularly with regard to matters of rhythm and tempo fluctuation, vibrato and portamento.[36] Fritz Kreisler (1875–1962) was the first to record Beethoven's Violin Concerto. Recorded between 14 and 16 December 1926, his performance with the Berlin State Opera Orchestra and Leo Blech is one of the principal landmarks in the history of recording, testifying to the remarkable grace and poise of his playing, his accomplished technique, musicianly phrasing, warm vibrant tone, subtlety of expression and characteristic use of portamento and rubato. Although Jascha Heifetz's (1901–88) slick solo playing (Boston Symphony Orchestra/Charles Munch) exhibits remarkable technical mastery and poise, his interpretation lacks the breadth of Kreisler's and Georg Kulenkampff's (1898–1948). Despite some technical shortcomings, Kulenkampff's recording with Hans Schmidt-Isserstedt and the Berlin Philharmonic Orchestra was long considered to be among the best as 'a musician's performance suffused with a classical serenity'.[37]

Carl Flesch believed that Joseph Szigeti was better '"canned" than live'.[38] Szigeti recorded Beethoven's Violin Concerto three times, twice with Bruno Walter at the helm (1932 and 1947), but his recording at the age of seventy-two with the London Symphony Orchestra and Antal Dorati, though not technically flawless, is undoubtedly his most communicative performance. Zino Francescatti's (1902–91) collaboration with the eighty-five–year-old Walter and the Columbia Symphony Orchestra is the most highly regarded of his three major recordings of the concerto. Walter also conducted the Flesch disciple Henryk Szeryng's (1918–88) debut with the Beethoven concerto in Warsaw, but Szeryng later made three acclaimed recordings of the work, that with Haitink and the Concertgebouw Orchestra (1973) best demonstrating his suave technique, intellectual phrasing and mature artistry. The Concertgebouw Orchestra was also involved (with Colin Davis) in Arthur Grumiaux's (1921–86) third recording of the work, characterised by his polished technique, relaxed lyricism, shapely phrasing and classical poise.

Adolf Busch (1891–1952; New York Philharmonic/Fritz Busch) offers essentially a Classical view of Beethoven's concerto tempered by a Romantic sensibility. His protégé Yehudi Menuhin (b. 1916), who was widely acclaimed for the maturity of his Carnegie Hall performance of Beethoven's concerto as an eleven-year-old, did not record the work until August 1947 (Lucerne Festival Orchestra/Furtwängler). However, Menuhin's most acclaimed Beethoven recording is his version with Klemperer and the New Philharmonia Orchestra, which represents a compromise between his impulsive romanticism and the conductor's austere, classical approach.

Of David Oistrakh's (1908–74) three versions, that with the Orchestre National de la Radiodiffusion Française/André Cluytens was his own preference, and this is supported by general critical opinion, on account of his strong aristocratic reading and impeccable phrasing and sense of line. The leaner, more aggressive approach of Leonid Kogan (1924–82) is reflected in his collaboration with Kirill Kondrashin and the State Orchestra of the USSR, combining power, nobility and introspection 'with an admirable feeling for stylistic integrity'.[39] The younger generation of Soviet violinists, among them Oistrakh's son Igor (b. 1931), Valéry Klimov (b. 1931) and latterly Gidon Kremer (b. 1947) and Dmitri Sitkovetsky (b. 1954), has yet to produce an outstanding recording of Beethoven's Violin Concerto. Kremer's two recordings of the work (Academy of St Martin in the Fields/Marriner; Chamber Orchestra of Europe/Harnoncourt), for example, are somewhat mannered and have suffered criticism because they incorporate controversial cadenzas by Schnittke and 'Beethoven/Kremer'.

Commencing with Albert Spalding (1888–1953; Austrian Symphony Orchestra/Loibner), the American contribution focuses on Isaac Stern (b. 1920; New York Philharmonic Orchestra/Bernstein) and the numerous distinguished pupils of Ivan Galamian, most notably Itzhak Perlman (b. 1945), Pinchas Zukerman (b. 1948) and Kyung-Wha Chung (b. 1948). Perlman's live recording (1986) of the concerto (Berlin Philharmonic Orchestra/Barenboim) marries depth of musical insight with technical mastery and individual expression, while Zukerman's highly disciplined reading with Mehta and the Los Angeles Philharmonic Orchestra is normally considered the best of his three recordings. Kyung-Wha Chung also adopts a surprisingly restrained, disciplined, 'Classical' approach to the work in combination with Kirill Kondrashin and the Vienna Philharmonic Orchestra, while her live recording with Tennstedt and the Amsterdam Concertgebouw Orchestra is quite the opposite, its outer movements full of flair and spontaneity and the Larghetto beautifully done.

The Austrian Wolfgang Schneiderhan (b. 1915) has been described as an 'antivirtuoso', who 'has an uncommon sense of style, at his best in Beethoven and Brahms'.[40] His interpretations of Beethoven's concerto rate very highly, his recording (1953) with Paul van Kempen and the Berlin Philharmonic Orchestra arguably being preferable to his later version (1962) with Eugen Jochum and the Berlin Philharmonic Orchestra, which has nevertheless been hailed as one of the greatest ever recordings of this concerto.[41] Among the postwar generation of German violinists, the talents of Anne-Sophie Mutter (b. 1963) have come to the fore, not least through the efforts of Herbert von Karajan and the Berlin Philharmonic Orchestra.

The publication of the facsimile of the autograph score in 1979 has already prompted Christian Tetzlaff (SWF-Sinfonieorchester Baden Baden/Gielen) to record the concerto incorporating some of its numerous alternative readings. The appendix of Herttrich's critical report for volume III/4 of the new Beethoven collected edition (Bonn and Munich, 1994) will doubtless prompt other violinists to explore further the provisionality of the solo part, such that the work, in future, may never seem quite the same. Furthermore, the revitalisation of early music performance has led to the release of competing period-instrument versions of the concerto by Stephanie Chase (Hanover Band/Goodman) and Monica Huggett (The Orchestra of the Age of Enlightenment/Mackerras), both recordings involving detailed scholarly work on the text and preparation of stylishly appropriate cadenzas.

Editions of the solo violin part

The place of Beethoven's Concerto in the forefront of the violin repertory is verified by the numerous editions of the violin part (with piano accompaniment) that have appeared since Joachim's championing of the work in the mid nineteenth century. These editions provide us with a wide and sometimes bewildering range of proposed solutions to the many details and inconsistencies that Beethoven left unresolved, as well as offering editorial suggestions regarding matters of technique, interpretation and performance practice.[42] As Alberto Bachmann has remarked: 'There are not two violinists in the world who interpret this work in the same manner, and it may be said with entire frankness, that many are guilty of crimes against art in allowing themselves liberties in its interpretation which would have shocked Beethoven himself...The various editions of this work also display a tendency to improve upon it which may truly be deplored...'[43] Bachmann illustrates from memory just a few of the liberties taken in respect of the opening three solo bars of the concerto by Joachim, Wilhelmj, Sarasate, Ysaÿe, Thomson, Kreisler, and Kubelík, examples ranging from the somewhat insensitive version ascribed to Wilhelmj, through the rather more articulated and accented interpretations of Thomson and Kreisler to the more faithful (to the original) versions of Joachim and Ysaÿe (Ex. 3.1).

Most editions of, or commentaries on, the solo violin part reflect the technical and interpretative practices of their respective eras. Some are particularly interventionist, providing a first-hand record of the interpretation of a fêted virtuoso (for example, those of Joachim himself, Ferdinand David, August Wilhelmj, Jenö Hubay and Joseph Szigeti) or teacher (notably those of Jacob Dont, Leopold Auer and Carl Flesch), and therefore require much care in interpretation. Dont's edition (Berlin, c1880), probably most closely approximates to early-nineteenth-century Viennese practice; others, like that of Heinrich Dessauer, which incorporates 'explanatory remarks for concert performance with special reference to the artistic conception of Joseph Joachim', offer information second-hand. Add to these the further source materials provided by writers of standard texts about violin technique and interpretation,[44] and the increasing availability nowadays of historical recordings, and it is possible to verify whether or not some of our editors actually practised what they preached!

On the other hand, the so-called *Urtext* of Willy Hess (1969), for example, concentrates on the provision of the text, with little in the way of editorial apparatus;[45] and Max Rostal steers a middle course between 'an original text which, as it stands, provides only a bare outline of the composer's ideas of instrumental execution, and...an edition, which fails to indicate where important additions or modifications have been made'. Beethoven's corrections and variants (clearly distinguished and without any editorial modification) are incorporated in the violin part of Rostal's piano score, 'to give violinists the opportunity to follow Beethoven's trend of thoughts and development'; however, following for the most part the first printed edition, Rostal also suggests his own fingerings and

43

3.1 Beethoven: Violin Concerto in D major Op. 61 (1st movement: Bachmann)

bowings as well as some additional dynamic markings (in brackets) in the separate solo violin part.[46]

Ferdinand David's editions of Beethoven's violin sonatas, piano trios, string quartets and Violin Concerto, as well as his arrangements of the cello sonatas for violin and piano, are the earliest systematically bowed and fingered editions of these works. Though his edition of the Concerto was published around 1870, the style of performance suggested by his annotations is likely to have much in common with the playing styles of Beethoven's latter years, particularly as David was a pupil of Spohr, one of the earliest violinists outside Vienna to champion Beethoven's Op. 18 quartets and violin sonatas.[47] Substantially accurate with respect to note lengths and pitches, though there are inevitably oversights and deliberate alterations, David's edition incorporates numerous differences in phrasing and articulation from the principal sources. In many cases, as Brown observes, 'the score contains one version (usually identical or almost identical with that of the *Gesamtausgabe*) while the violin part has another', suggesting probably an attempt on David's part to offer a more practicable solution, for example, to the knotty problem of interpreting Beethoven's impossibly long slurs (an indication of legato rather than specific bowing) or to indicate individual preferences concerning bow strokes and articulation.[48]

Many editors throughout the years have been fairly faithful to what Beethoven wrote or evidently sanctioned. A few, however, have attempted to 'improve' musically on Beethoven's text(s) by adding or changing notes (e.g. Wilhelmj, David, Dont and Szigeti), modifying rhythms (e.g. Flesch and Wilhelmj), or adding expressive terminology and/or dynamic markings foreign to the various primary sources (e.g. Joachim and Moser, Auer, Hubay and Wilhelmj), in most cases failing to distinguish between their own and Beethoven's markings.[49] The lack of agreement amongst editors over bowings and articulations is perfectly understandable, especially considering the incidence of Beethoven's long 'phrasing slurs', the chaotic state of the autograph itself and its relationship to the other principal sources with regard to slurring, and the contrasting performing styles embraced by the various editions. Dont's edition, the preface of which suggests that it may reflect most closely Clement's interpretation of the work, offers us some clues as to his modifications to the articulations of Beethoven's autograph, thereby supporting the hypothesis that Beethoven himself sanctioned such alterations and intended his annotated bowings and articulations only as a rough guide for the soloist. There is no better example of a passage on whose bowing editors almost always beg to differ than 1/134–41, where, as Bachmann confirms, 'every violinist uses a different bowing'.[50] Some versions of this passage include slurring patterns which offer variety

3.2 Beethoven: Violin Concerto in D major Op. 61 (1st movement: Clement –
according to Moser)

3.3 Beethoven: Violin Concerto in D major Op. 61 (1st movement: ed. David)

3.4 Beethoven: Violin Concerto in D major Op. 61 (1st movement: ed. Dont)

and comfort, while many seem designed more for the purpose of bravura
display, most notably the so-called 'Paganini bowing'. Moser, writing
about 'Viennese traditions' in violin playing, relates: 'Certainly Joachim
told me that already during his time of study with Joseph Böhm[sic] the
opinion was widespread among the Viennese violinists that Franz
Clement, at the first performance of the Beethoven Violin Concerto
...had already used the aforesaid ['Paganini'] bowing at the following
place in the first movement' (Ex. 3.2).[51] This bowing is very similar to
that employed by David (Ex. 3.3) for the same passage but somewhat
different from Dont's version (Ex. 3.4). As Brown concludes: 'Assum-
ing that Moser's "traditions" and Dont's preface can be relied on, this
raises the possibility that Clement (presumably with Beethoven's con-
currence) later changed his treatment of the passage. But whatever patterns of bowing Beethoven may directly have sanctioned, the
implication that he expected some of the passages of separate notes to
receive this kind of treatment seems irresistible.'[52]

Two particular developments in nineteenth-century interpretation were the increased prominence given to the cultivation of an expressive singing style, with the strong tone and broad or *martelé* bow strokes characteristic of the Parisian violin school of Viotti and his contemporaries, and a greater virtuoso element. These developments are reflected in the various editions of Beethoven's Concerto by addition of appropriate terminology and slurs (particularly the so-called 'overlapping slur', which traverses the beat), the increased use of portato, broad *détaché* and 'hooked' strokes, as well as in attitudes towards fingering, notably the use of portamento, and una corda playing for the cultivation of tonal uniformity. However, the expressive potential of harmonics, glissandos and portamentos, milked unflinchingly by most late-nineteenth-century editors and performers, has not entered so readily into the vocabulary of the violinists of the current century, many of whom advocate the use of extensions to eliminate shifts and avoid 'slides' and favour, where practicable, the lower, more fundamental left-hand positions to cultivate cleaner and clearer articulation.

The version for piano Op. 61a

In 1802, Muzio Clementi, the English composer, keyboard player and teacher, music publisher and piano manufacturer of Italian birth, embarked on his third European tour. On this occasion he travelled as a representative of his firm of Clementi, Banger, Hyde, Collard and Davis, with the principal aims of cultivating markets for Clementi pianos and negotiating with composers and publishers for rights to new music. He visited Vienna four times during his tour (1802, 1804, 1806–7, 1808–10), but evidently did not succeed in meeting Beethoven formally until 1807. Wegeler reports:

> When Clementi came to Vienna Beethoven wanted to go to see him at once but his brother put it into his head that it was for Clementi to call first. Though much the older man, the latter would probably have done so, if there had not been so much foolish talk about it. In the end he spent a long time in Vienna without getting to know Beethoven except by sight. Many a time at mid-day they actually sat at the same table at The Swan, Clementi with his pupil Klengel and Beethoven with me: we all knew one another but neither party said a word to the other or at most passed the time of day.[53]

When at last the two met, Clementi was successful in securing the exclusive English rights to some of Beethoven's music, signing a contract with him on 20 April 1807 for six major works: the three 'Rasumovsky' Quartets Op. 59; the Fourth Symphony Op. 60; the Overture to Coriolan Op. 62; the Fourth Piano Concerto Op. 58; the Violin Concerto Op. 61; and an arrangement of this latter concerto for the pianoforte 'with additional notes'. Although the political situation caused complications in both the dispatch of all the music to London and the payment for it and Clementi never published the Fourth Symphony, Fourth Piano Concerto or Coriolan Overture, the agreement eventually became the basis for a continuing, mutually beneficial arrangement. Clementi's firm published the Op. 59 Quartets in 1809–10, by which time another London publisher had already seen them into print; and the edition of the Violin Concerto and its arrangement for piano appeared in the autumn of 1810. Meanwhile, all six works had been published in Vienna by 1808. But in 1810–11 Clementi & Co. issued first editions of ten new works by Beethoven – Opp. 73–82 – all of which made their appearance in London for the first time anywhere.[54]

Piano transcriptions of violin concertos were fairly common at that time; several of Viotti's violin concertos, for example, were arranged for piano by eminent pianists such as Steibelt and Dussek.[55] Similarly, a large number of Beethoven's works were arranged for other media in order to make them more widely available to an eager public. As Barry Cooper points out, Beethoven may previously have contemplated adapting for piano a work originally conceived for the violin; the existence of a piano cadenza in G which is thematically related to the surviving fragment of the early Violin Concerto in C WoO5 certainly lends credibility to such an assertion.[56]

Clementi had written enthusiastically to Collard about his deal with Beethoven: 'Remember that the Violin Concerto he will adapt himself and end it as soon as he can.'[57] However, doubts have been raised as to whether this version is actually by Beethoven, as he evidently had relatively little interest in the task of transcription and often left such arrangements to pupils such as Ries and Czerny, merely checking their work and making minor alterations himself.[58] In the transcription, the orchestration is unaltered. Fritz Kaiser suggests that Beethoven's contribution to the solo piano part was minimal, a plausible view in spite of the four cadenzas in the composer's hand;[59] but the weight of available evidence suggests that Beethoven either undertook the piano adaptation himself or, at least, made extensive prescriptions, largely of the left-hand part (for the substance of the right-hand contribution is incorporated, with only slight divergences, in the solo violin part), in the autograph for a copyist/pupil to follow. The former alternative is perhaps more likely, because, in 1816, Beethoven is known to have given the pianist Charles Neate (1784–1877) a copy of the score with an arrangement of the solo part for piano on the same pages, claiming that he himself had written and played it.[60] He is also known to have checked the *Stichvorlage* from which the Viennese first editions of both versions were engraved, and made a few proof-stage corrections.

However, this may be a forced argument, for as Tyson writes: 'Anyone who wants to defend Beethoven's full authorship should at any rate ask himself why there are no chords in the piano's right hand – a form of abstinence renounced by the Beethoven who wrote the cadenzas. And he should look at the broken-backed adaptation of the coda of the first movement, particularly bars 511–23.'[61] Furthermore, many of the accompanying figures for the piano's left hand, most of which accord with the suggestions added to the autograph, are surprisingly banal and unimaginative, comprising largely chords and single notes, accompanying figures (mostly in broken triads) and numerous octave doublings of the right-hand part. However, the accompanying figure for the main rondo theme is somewhat more appropriate and the highly original cadenza for the first movement is a *tour de force* of pianism. Beethoven's correspondence of the summer of 1807 informs us that he was anxious to despatch the transcription commissioned by Clementi and was, because of this and ill-health, falling behind in the completion of another important commission, the Mass in C.[62] Thus, he might have been tempted to call on others for assistance in amplifying his sketched ideas for the piano version. In any case, one assumes that, as Beethoven checked and corrected the transcription, it must have met with his approval and should be recognised as his work.

Pianists have almost completely neglected Op. 61a, largely because it is 'highly unsatisfactory'[63] and because Beethoven's five other piano concertos are in their various different ways so much more fulfilling. One wonders, however, whether it would be quite so maligned if listeners were not so familiar with the 'original' version for violin.

49

4

The textual history

The autograph of Beethoven's concerto bears the amusing inscription 'Concerto par Clemenza pour Clement, primo Violino e Direttore al theatro a Vienne, dal L.v.Bthvn. 1806', Tovey calling this 'a virile pun on his "clemency" towards the poor composer'.[1] However, the work was dedicated not to Clement but to Beethoven's childhood friend Stephan von Breuning and was first published in Vienna. The year of publication is normally given as 1808, but evidence suggests that it was certainly available by August 1807. It appeared at about the same time as its adaptation for piano, which, dedicated to von Breuning's wife, Julie, was announced along with the Fourth Piano Concerto in the *Wiener Zeitung* of 10 August 1808.

Sketches

Beethoven is known to have recorded his ideas as soon as possible in sketchbooks, which appear gradually to have become indispensable to his creative process, especially the planning and re-planning of structural procedures and the progressive refinement of thematic material. They were very personal documents that remained with Beethoven throughout his life, in excess of fifty being included in the auction of his *Nachlass*.[2]

Beethoven's method of working on several compositions concurrently resulted in those few sketches that have survived for his Violin Concerto being intermingled with those for his Fifth Symphony and the Cello Sonata Op. 69. It is difficult to believe that no other sketches were made for such a complex work and it seems more likely that a single book of sketches has been lost than that several loose leaves have gone astray. Barry Cooper notes that there is a similar situation for works of late 1799 and early 1800, including the Quartet Op. 18 No. 4, the Septet Op. 20, the First Symphony and the Third Piano Concerto. He later points out that if one defines a sketch as any version of part of a work that precedes the final version, then the autographs are full of sketches, most incorporating modifications such as deletions, alterations, additions, discarded leaves and inserted leaves.[3] The cue-staff, of which there are numerous examples in the autograph of the Violin Concerto, is really a type of sketch and doubtless served as an invaluable guide to Beethoven when planning the layout of the score, enabling him to integrate his ideas, balance the proportions of the different parts of a movement or section and maintain a sense of continuity.

Principal sources

Four principal sources have attracted the particular attention of editors who have sought to establish the text of the concerto, taking into consideration both the violin version and its transcription for piano:[4]

A. The autograph score, housed in the Nationalbibliothek, Vienna (H.S. 17538);[5]

B. A full score in the hand of a copyist, housed in the British Library (Add. MS 47 851);

C. The first edition (parts only), published by the Kunst- und Industriekontor, Vienna, c1808;

D. An edition (parts only) published by Clementi & Co., London, in 1810.

Of the set of orchestral parts used at the first performance on 23 December 1806, only a fragment of the first oboe part is extant; this, comprising the last sixty-one bars of the first movement, is housed in the Library of Congress, Washington.

The autograph (A), claims Tyson, 'represents the first full-scale writing-down of the work; and – as is so often found in Beethoven autographs – it exhibits at the same time the final stages of composition',[6] not least, apparently, Beethoven's indecision (see Fig. 4.1). It also backs up Czerny's comments about the great speed of the work's composition, especially of the finale, and the fact that it was premiered barely two days after it had been completed.[7] The orchestral parts, though subjected to substantial modifications, are more or less in their final forms as we know them, but the solo violin part, written on a staff near the bottom of the

Figure 4.1 Page from the autograph of Beethoven's Violin Concerto Op. 61
(3rd movement, bars 77-82)

score, is not. Under it appear the two staves for the cellos (left blank in
'col bassi' passages) and basses, and under these are three unassigned
additional staves. On one of these three blank staves – usually the middle
one – and very occasionally on more than one, Beethoven has written
alternative versions for several solo passages. The variants in the additional middle staff are written in the same light brown ink as the main
solo staff and would appear to be corrections, since they generally replace
crossed-out bars in the solo staff. The other variants, marked by a cross
and written in darker ink, appear to be either alternatives or improve-
ments to the unblemished version on the main solo stave. Thus, two, and
sometimes three, versions of the solo part co-exist for a substantial pro-
portion of the work – more than one third of the solo part of the first
movement and over one quarter of the finale.

The full score (B), complete except for the first page (four bars), is in
the hand of a copyist – Tyson suggests Wenzel Schlemmer as a likely
scribe. The copyist's errors and misreadings suggest that the orchestral
parts were copied from the autograph (A), but the solo violin part

together with the solo piano part for Op. 61a appear here for the first time in their final forms, the violin below the piano. The sixteen staves are assigned in the following order (from top to bottom): Violin I, Violin II, Viola, Flauto, Oboi, Clarinetti, Fagotti, Corni, Trombe, Timpani, Pianoforte (two staves), an empty staff, Violino principale, Violoncelli (the staff being used only when the cello part differs from that of the bassi), Bassi. How these final versions were produced, however, remains a mystery, as no manuscript sources from which the copyist transcribed the two solo parts have survived. Naturally, one wonders whether as many errors were introduced in the solo parts as, indeed, infiltrated the orchestral parts in the copyist's version.

This source also includes numerous additions and corrections in Beethoven's hand, in pencil (mostly inked over, perhaps by the copyist) or in his famous Rötel (red crayon), involving largely annotations of expression, dynamics, phrasing and accidentals. There are also bold check-marks in red crayon on every page at the beginning of each staff, except those of the solo violin and the trumpets; occasionally, a 'squiggle' appears across the staff of a single part, usually with a number beside it. The location of the squiggles corresponds to the line- and page-endings of the first edition (both versions) of Op. 61 (Source C) and seems to confirm that this source served as *Stichvorlage*, the score from which the separate parts were copied by the engraver. Tyson suggests that the check-marks were probably made by Beethoven during the proof-reading stage. He further claims that Beethoven's pencilled corrections were inserted *before* the score was sent to the engraver, and that his entries in red crayon were made *after* the parts had been engraved but before they were issued, i.e. at the proof stage. Examination of the parts in those places where changes in red crayon have been made in the score reveals that the plates have been modified to accommodate the change (indicated by irregularity in the engraving, or, in the case of the addition of expression markings etc., by the use of a different engraving punch, clef, or lettering style). The pencilled changes, however, have not necessitated changes on the plates and were therefore entered in Source B before it was used for the engraving of the parts.[8]

The first edition of the parts (Source C) of the concerto in both forms is based on Source B, save for the trumpet parts and the solo violin part; however, the solo violin parts of B and C are not especially divergent.[9]

Tyson observes both the lack of check-marks at the beginning of each staff of the solo violin part in B and the fact that the squiggles do not correspond entirely to B's page-endings. He goes on to suggest that the squiggles might correspond to the page-endings in a manuscript copy of the part, now lost, and that this lost copy was the *Vorlage* for the first edition.

The London edition of the violin concerto (Source D), published by Clementi & Co. in the summer of 1810, has survived in a single set of parts housed in the Royal College of Music, London. One copy of the piano version also survives, divided between the Royal College of Music (solo part) and the British Library (orchestral parts).[10] Tyson clarifies the textual status of this source, proving that the orchestral parts are textually quite inedependent of Source C – they do not incorporate, for example, the corrections or alterations that Beethoven marked in pencil or crayon – and that they were based on a manuscript set of parts copied directly from Source A.[11] The solo parts of Source D, however, seem to be derived textually from the solo part of C and incorporate numerous errors.

As the autograph obviously represents something short of the composer's final intentions, familiarity with Sources A, B, C and D has enabled editors to produce an accurate text for certain passages of the work; furthermore, it has also enabled them both to understand how the various textual corruptions have occurred in those parts of the autograph that are unsatisfactory and to decide upon an appropriate course of action.

The text

The textual history of this concerto is extraordinarily complex in that the solo part that has come down to us, though based largely on the material of the autograph, incorporates further different versions of its own. Opinions differ regarding the origins and interpretation of these variants. Otto Jahn regards the autograph variants in darker ink as constituting a new, re-worked version made under Clement's guidance before the premiere. He speculates that Beethoven initially respected Clement's advice on technical matters but later re-instated many of his original ideas. Nottebohm also focuses on technical considerations, believing that the degree of technical difficulty for the soloist prompted Beethoven to re-write his 'corrected version.' He concludes that 'while some parts become easier to play as a result of these changes, others lose their musical significance', a possible explanation, he claims, why the version for piano follows largely the violin part on the main solo staff. Oswald Jonas, however, attributes the changes in the autograph to the fact that the pianistic origins of the solo part made it fundamentally unsuited to the violin.[12]

While Jahn, Nottebohm and Jonas are firmly of the opinion that the version of the solo part known to us nowadays was written and approved by Beethoven, Fritz Kaiser doubts its authenticity, citing the lack of proof that it was printed or corrected with Beethoven's approval. He suggests that 'it amounts to a parody of the original text' and derides its confused, disjointed style and illogicality, which, he claims, are uncharacteristic of the composer. He attributes both this version and that of the piano adaptation to Alexander Pössinger. Willy Hess shares Kaiser's doubts about the version's authenticity, largely because 'uncertainty must remain as long as one manuscript is missing'; but he agrees with his predecessors that Beethoven wrote the autograph's variants in darker ink after collaborating with Clement, who found the original too difficult and unviolinistic, and that this represents a complete, re-worked version.[13]

Shin Kojima acknowledges the plausibility of all the above arguments at first sight but claims that none stands up to close scrutiny. His investigations focus on the following five issues:

1. which version Clement played at the work's premiere;
2. whether Clement influenced Beethoven or, if so, on which version they collaborated;
3. when Beethoven entered the version in darker ink into the autograph;
4. whether this version actually constitutes a self-contained version;
5. whether the authenticity of the solo part that has come down to us is really as doubtful as Kaiser claims.[14]

In his attempts to establish the dates for each version, and hence provide answers for 1–3 above, Kojima reveals that Beethoven spent the months of September and October 1806 at Grätz Castle near Troppau as the guest of Prince Carl von Lichnowsky. The single existing sketch of the concerto possibly dates from his time at the castle, as the paper has the same watermark and three crescents as that of the autograph of the Piano Sonata Op. 57. However, it is unlikely that he started work on the autograph score during this stay, largely because it would have been written, at least in part, in the darker ink of his letter to Breitkopf & Härtel of 3 September 1806; and neither this letter nor one written on his return to Vienna (18 November 1806) mentions the Violin Concerto.[15] Only Opp. 58, 59 and 60 are specified, suggesting that if Beethoven started work on the concerto in late November, he must have completed it in about four to five weeks, confirming contemporary reports that it was written in a short time.

Studies of Beethoven's letters reveal that the period during which both types of ink were used spanned the end of April to the beginning of May 1807, light brown ink being used until about 26 April 1807,[16] and dark brown being employed certainly from 11 May 1807.[17] With regard to his compositions, an approximate period may be defined for Beethoven's use of light brown (for Opp. 59 No. 3, 60, 61 and 62; August 1806 to February 1807) and dark brown ink (for Op. 86, from July/August 1807, and the revision to the 'corrected' version of the Violin Concerto). Kojima therefore concludes that the variants in darker ink must have been added after the concerto's premiere. Furthermore, Beethoven's additional pencil drafts for the solo piano part must postdate his commission from Clementi to adapt the concerto for piano (20 April 1807), suggesting that he began revising his 'corrected' version later than the pencil drafts for the piano transcription (later than April 1807) but before he completed the piano version.

The autograph's orchestra parts also include subsequent additions in both dark ink and pencil. These additions, unlike those in red crayon, are not incorporated into Clementi's edition of the parts (D), which mirrors the early version of the autograph. According to Clementi, the *Stichvorlage* for his edition was sent to his partner Collard in London on 22 April 1807, only two days after the commission had been made.[18] It would therefore scarcely have been possible for Beethoven to write out a completely new score for this venture, nor would he have had any reason to do so. Kojima therefore concludes that the additions to the orchestral parts of the original autograph, its variants in darker ink and the pencil sketches for the piano version were added at the end of April 1807 at the earliest, and thus at least four months after the completion of the original autograph score and its lighter-ink variants premiered by Clement on 23 December 1806. Clement may not, in fact, have collaborated with Beethoven in the subsequent revision process. Had he done so, claims Kojima, it would have been possible only in connection with the version premiered and this is unlikely given the unviolinistic idiom of much of the solo part. Kojima adds that as Beethoven wrote the concerto, according to his dedication, 'out of pity for Clement', it is unlikely that he needed Clement's assistance.

Kojima's convincing argument that Beethoven regarded the version premiered by Clement as a complete and final version of the concerto and had no qualms about sending it to London for Clementi to publish leads him to further conclusions which either disprove those of other scholars or suggest new theories. He dismisses Nottebohm's assumption that Beethoven fell back on the premiered version to save his original, musically more significant or more pianistic concept, pointing out that Beethoven evidently began writing down the draft for the left hand of the piano version in the autograph at the end of April 1807, at which time only the premiered version had been written. He further argues that it was Beethoven's work on the piano transcription that caused him to question the appropriateness of some of the violin part and to make alterations accordingly on the empty staves. Kojima gives a detailed and convincing analysis of Beethoven's correction methods in selected sections of the autograph and suggests that, because these alterations multiplied during the course of the process, Beethoven left all the variants in place in order to make a final decision at a later stage. He therefore concludes that the parallel existence of the premiered version (in lighter ink) and the darker-ink variants on the autograph represent not so much equal alternatives as an interim stage of the re-writing process, of which the version known nowadays is the finished product.

Attempts to date this finished product have proved inconclusive. However, by taking various letters and other sources into account, tracing Beethoven's involvement in the correction process for the first printed edition and bearing in mind that the January 1808 issue of the *Weimar Journal des Luxus und der Moden* mentioned that the Violin Concerto as well as Opp. 59, 60 and 62 were already in print in August 1807,

Kojima suggests that Source B (i.e. British Library Add. MS 47 851) was used as a print copy for C (Vienna print) by the middle of July at the latest and that the version of the concerto as we now know it (and the piano version) probably dates from May–June 1807.

Finally, Kojima embarks on a detailed 'morphological examination' of the sources in order to disprove Kaiser's doubts regarding the authenticity of the solo part known to us nowadays. He concludes that this version can be shown to have grown out of the continuation and enhancement of the version with variants in darker ink, which in turn was a re-worked version of the original premiered version. While this latter constitutes a thought-through self-contained version, that in darker ink does not, as its variants are mainly sketches for improvement of the original. Although these versions in the autograph often run parallel and neither is crossed out, it should not be interpreted that Beethoven viewed them as alternatives in their own right. Such ambiguity only arose because the autograph, which at the time of re-writing had lost its original status of clean copy, had been reduced essentially to sketchbook status by Beethoven, forming the starting-point for the harmoniously integrated version of the work familiar to us nowadays.

Beethoven's concerto is 'as problematic from a textual point of view as it is central to its genre',[19] for, contrary to his violin sonatas, his final intentions are at times ambiguous as regards pitches and rhythms, and dynamics, phrasing, articulation and other such annotations have been left in a very incomplete form. Many of these ambiguities arise from the efforts of editors to correct perceived errors on Beethoven's part, for, as Tyson observes, there are several passages 'in which recourse to the autograph, although illuminating, can yet be at the same time disappointing, since it will show us, in effect, that Beethoven was not particularly concerned to make up his mind about a detail or to resolve an inconsistency.'[20] Furthermore, errors in Source B confirm that Beethoven was not a good proof-reader; he seems to have had a sharp eye for missing accidentals and clef-changes, but allowed more serious errors to escape him. Thus, many of Beethoven's errors in the autograph have been perpetuated and added to during the concerto's journey through the copyist's score to its first engraved edition. Norman Del Mar and Alan Tyson have exposed several textual problems associated with the work, Tyson in particular examining a number of these corruptions in detail and showing that they 'are certainly as old as the first edition of 1808.'[21] Although it is beyond the scope of this volume to provide a comprehensive survey of the numerous textual problems associated with this concerto, Appendix 3 pinpoints some of the most significant errors, inconsistencies and dubious passages which have been perpetuated and challenged.

5

Structure and style I–
1. Allegro ma non troppo

With his Third Piano Concerto (*c*1800), Beethoven had begun to free himself from many contemporary conventions in the genre. He had broadened the scope of the first movement to symphonic proportions, combining thematic development with the free fantasia of the French concerto; he had restored and strengthened the principle of equality and opposition between orchestra and soloist; and he had achieved a much greater concentration, integration and economy of thematic material, shared by orchestra and soloist. He built upon these developments in his Violin Concerto. Despite its implied march pulse, the first movement is far removed from the concerto concept of Beethoven's contemporaries, whose thematic and formal freedom is replaced by a more tightly-knit symphonic structure on the largest scale. Greater emphasis is placed on thematic development and structural coherence and less weight on virtuoso display, the soloist appearing at times almost incidental and functioning more as a commentator upon and embellisher of thematic statements and developments made by the orchestra than as a means of developing that material or introducing new themes. As Georges Enesco perceptively remarked: 'This is a great symphony. The violin has a leading voice, but it is merely one of the many orchestral voices which make up the whole.'[1]

Beethoven's skill and ingenuity in orchestration yield a rich kaleidoscope of orchestral colour, in which the ever-varied contrasts and combinations of solo violin and woodwind have particular significance. Much of the thematic material contributed by the orchestra is scored for the woodwind, especially the flute, oboe or clarinet, in preference to the strings, simply because these instruments offer a better contrast to the timbre of the soloist. The extent to which the winds are used in the first movement's opening ritornello is a case in point, string colour being

---

reserved largely for the entry of the soloist, who reciprocates with predominantly lyrical material exploiting the higher registers of the instrument. Such concentration on the instrument's higher reaches clearly separates the soloist in range from the orchestral violins and allows this voice more effectively to penetrate full-textured passages of orchestral accompaniment.

Although the overall effect of the movement is one of solid foundations of harmonic stasis, harmonic activity at the surface level shows much greater imagination and complexity. Charles Rosen draws a comparison between Beethoven's first movement and that of Mozart's Piano Concerto in C K.503, observing that both use a similar emphasis on the root of the tonic triad and a series of changes from major to minor for their 'expansive effect of power and tenderness'.[2] The predominance of the tonic is clearly evident from the analytical outline of the movement provided in Table 5.1. Well over half the movement's 535 bars show such tonal affiliations; and Beethoven's skilful juxtaposition of the tonic major and minor is exemplified almost immediately with his treatment of the second theme, which is prepared in the minor mode and announced in the major (woodwind, b. 43). Eight bars later, the violins repeat and enlarge upon it in D minor; not until b. 73 does the major mode finally re-establish itself prior to the soloist's first entry.

Tovey's description of Beethoven's Violin Concerto as 'gigantic' and 'one of the most spacious concertos ever written'[3] is largely due to the vast dimensions of its first movement, which, in achieving a complete reconciliation of concerto and sonata-form principles, conforms to the structural outline presented in Table 5.1.

1–88 Ritornello 1

In keeping with his mature practice of introducing an important motif on the timpani – for example, in the first movement of the Third Piano Concerto, the finales of the Fifth and Seventh Symphonies and the scherzo of Symphony No. 9 – Beethoven opens the first movement with a five-stroke timpani figure. Andreas Moser relates:

> The idea of this curious *motive* is said to have occurred to Beethoven during the stillness of a sleepless night, on hearing someone knocking at the door of a neighbouring house. The knocking consisted always of five

Table 5.1 *Outline structure of Allegro ma non troppo (sonata-form designations in brackets)*

Bars			
1–88	Ritornello 1	(Tutti exposition)	D major/D minor
89–223	First solo	(Solo exposition)	D major – A major
224–283	Ritornello 2	(Development)	[F major] A major/ A minor – C major
284–364	Second solo		C major – G minor
365–385	Ritornello 3	(Recapitulation)	D major
386–496	Third solo		
497–510	Ritornello 4		
510	Solo cadenza	(Solo cadenza)	
511–535	Coda	(Coda)	

regular blows in succession, repeated after a pause; and Beethoven, overjoyed at being able to distinguish the sound so clearly, for at this time his hearing was beginning to be seriously impaired, used it as the opening theme for the violin concerto with which he was then occupied. Thus these sounds, so prosaic in themselves, became for him the germ of a musical idea, from which, in the course of the movement, he evolved a wonderfully poetic meaning.[4]

Although the veracity of Moser's statement regarding the source of Beethoven's inspiration cannot be confirmed, the structural and poetic significance of this timpani motif is undeniable. Far from being a mere 'call to attention' for the audience, it serves as an essential developmental element and unifying device throughout the movement, appearing sometimes as a melodic idea, sometimes as a characteristic accompaniment to other themes, and occasionally with surprising harmonic changes and transformations. Rhythmic motifs involving repeated notes are also characteristic of other Beethoven works of the period, notably the first movements of the Waldstein and Appassionata Sonatas, the Fourth Piano Concerto and the Fifth Symphony. In these movements the repeated notes drive the music forwards as if acting as an anacrusis, but the Violin Concerto begins on a downbeat, anchoring the motif and ensuring its stability. Taking together the clearly defined occurrences outlined in Table 5.2 and various other disguised appearances (for

5.1 Beethoven: Violin Concerto in D major Op. 61 (1st movement),
illustrating the form in which the opening bars of the movement appeared in
the composer's sketchbook

example, the cello/bass phrase at bb. 87–8 and 282–3, taken up by violins
and violas to introduce the soloist, and the similar figure at bb. 392–3,
396–7), it is evident that the motif appears in some guise or other in over
one half of the movement's 535 bars, demonstrating remarkable
economy of means.

The radiant first theme (D major) is announced *dolce* in the woodwind
(bb. 2–9), punctuated in its midst by the timpani motif. It establishes not
only the predominantly lyrical qualities of the work but also a rhythmic
element (bb. 8–9) which is shared by two other significant ideas – the
second theme (bb. 43–50: see oboes, clarinets, bassoons in bb. 43, 45 and
47) and the ritornello's closing theme (bb. 77–86: see first violins in b. 78;
flute, clarinets, bassoons in b. 82; cellos and basses in bb. 80, 84; and
cellos/basses and bassoons in b. 85). An off-key gesture typical of
Beethoven follows the first theme's concluding perfect cadence in D
major. The first violins' *d♯*'s (b. 10) in that ubiquitous timpani rhythm
suddenly distort the feeling of the tonic key, which is just as quickly
clarified by the ensuing dominant seventh chord of D and the strings'
completion of the theme. Ex. 5.1 illustrates the form in which this idea
first appeared in the composer's sketchbook. Tovey explains:

> In Beethoven's first sketches he thought of the D sharp as E flat, a distinc-
> tion which, unnoticed on tempered instruments, is really important here.

E flat means something harmonically clearer, but the point about the D sharp is that it indeed is D sharp, though Beethoven leaves it unharmonised and carefully avoids letting it move in the direction which would explain it away. We shall see the explanation in one of the later phrases.[5]

A rising scale theme with an attendant downward leap is introduced by the first clarinet and first bassoon, confirming Beethoven's common usage of predominantly step-wise movement for the movement's thematic content. This scale theme is later reinforced first by the second clarinet and second bassoon, who double the line in thirds, and then by the oboes over an accompaniment which has affinities with the timpani figure. It rises to a peak and then quickly subsides in preparation for a typically Beethovenian dramatic gesture: a sudden, energetic *fortissimo* outburst in the remote key of B♭ major. In turn this spawns a passage in which the first violins, and sometimes the strings in full force, exploit incisively the rhythm of the timpani motive in diminution, supported by off-beat sforzandos. This rhythm persists until the timpani figure itself introduces the woodwind's announcement of the broad second theme in the tonic key (bb. 43–50), punctuating it throughout its major-mode course. This theme is immediately repeated and extended in the minor mode (violins), in a style later characteristic of Schubert, demonstrating the movement's major-minor ambivalence, which is emphasised colouristically within the orchestra (see also, for example, bb. 118–25 in the clarinets, bassoons, violins and violas, and bb. 126ff. in the solo violin). With the punctuating motto figure still very much in evidence (horns, trumpets and timpani), the melody is broadened somewhat by an accompanimental triplet figuration (violas and cellos). As the accompaniment becomes increasingly more complex, the woodwinds add their volume to the crescendo, after the climax of which the mystery of the repeated motto-like *d♯*'s, first featured at b. 10, is quietly and satisfactorily resolved by the strings' fully harmonised melodic version (bb. 65ff).

A gradual crescendo, underpinned by a bass-line possibly derived from the timpani figure, leads to the re-establishment of the tonic key with a majestic closing theme (b. 77) whose two-bar phrases alternate in dialogue between first violins (with woodwind reinforcements in the second strain) and cellos/basses. This melody, which bears close similarity to material heard at the beginning of Beethoven's Leonora Overture No. 1,[6] is the most constant of all, for it always follows a section devoted to the second subject and is, with one exception only, played by the same instruments. An extension of its last bar (bassoons, cellos/basses) incorporates an effective dramatic gesture, where, after three emphatic sforzandos, the orchestra dies away suddenly, outlining a dominant seventh chord of D to prepare for and overlap with the entry of the soloist – the soloist's entry is essentially an inversion of the previous two orchestral bars, which, in turn, find their derivation in bb. 24 and 25. Such an overlap, which Beethoven adopted increasingly in his later concertos, provides a greater sense of continuity than would result from the customary late-eighteenth-century perfect-cadence 'full stop' before the solo entry. With his cadenza-like opening solo passage, Beethoven here expands this ploy to such an extent that the dominant remains unresolved for fourteen bars.

89–223 First solo

The greater length and more symphonic nature of Beethoven's opening tuttis, particularly from the Third Piano Concerto onwards, naturally begged a suitably dramatic opening gesture from the soloist. The listener is not disappointed, as the solo violinist makes his sublime ascent in octaves, performs his striking quasi-extempore written-out elaborations on the dominant seventh chord and eventually resolves it on the tonic before embarking on his own exposition of the material, triggered by the timpani's motto figure (b. 101). A solo elaboration of the main theme follows, high in the violin's register, but supported by the woodwind and with the expected timpani strokes at the end of each phrase. Soloist and orchestra together work out all the themes seriatim in a remarkable enrichment of the preceding ritornello. Orchestral strings reiterate the timpani figure underneath solo passagework which never appears to be decoration for effect, but is all part of the invention's spontaneous flow.

The scale theme becomes a symphonic passage of transition, played initially by first clarinet and first bassoon in the major mode (bb. 118–19), then by clarinets and bassoons in thirds (bb. 120–1) and by the upper strings (bb. 122–5), and finally embellished in octaves by the soloist (bb. 126ff.), who, starting with a minor-mode version, manoeuvres it into new tonal directions. The equivalent of the surprise at b. 28 is reserved for another purpose; instead, the soloist ignores the gentle banter between wind and strings and contributes passagework which leads to the dominant chord of A major (b. 139) and eventually a solo trill on *e″* in preparation for a statement of the second theme in the dominant key (clarinets, bassoons). On this occasion, the timpani figure which accompanied this theme in the first ritornello is surprisingly absent. The soloist breaks off from his trill to take up and complete the theme's second phrase before embarking on figuration, comprising largely triplets in scales, broken octaves and somewhat angular arpeggios, which forms an ornamental background to an expanded, minor-mode version of the theme in the orchestra (mainly first violins and violas).

The soloist does not resume a melodic role again until b. 166, where reference is again made to the timpani figure (or the violin version, *a♯″* here) in its original and ornamental form. This leads to a brilliant climax, the soloist's majestic arpeggio figuration being punctuated by the orchestral strings before it peters out into a quiet recollection of the closing theme (b. 178), characterised initially by its two-bar contrasts of register. The cellos, and later the violins, first oboe and first clarinet expand it in rising sequences while the soloist contributes yet more semi-quaver scale and arpeggio elaboration in a long crescendo to a climactic passage in triplets at b. 195.

After a quiet chromatic scale on E, the solo line becomes more melodic, punctuated by the timpani motif in string guise. It concludes its excursion into the higher registers with a conventional trill, traditionally indicating the end of a major solo section and implying a perfect cadence in A major in preparation for an orchestral tutti (b. 205); but the entrance of the timpani figure (first violins) below the solo trill (b. 206) and the cellos' and basses' surprising low, *pianissimo* F♮ response (b. 207) remove us, albeit momentarily, from such tonal stability. The trill rises chromatically by step above this harmonic uncertainty, forming a chromatic fourth, the first of three instances of this device at significant structural points in the first movement (bb. 205–13, 351–7, and in the 'recapitulation' at bb. 479–87), all three increasing the drama by using the timpani motif as a counterpoint to the chromatic line. It is, as Peter Williams puts it, an old gesture used 'for maximum rhetoric',[7] and he believes that the first two examples are so different from each other in direction (rising/falling), texture (melodic/harmonic), position (soprano/bass), mode (major/minor), scoring (without/with bass) and in function (the first interrupts a cadence, the second leads to one) as to suggest conscious calculation on Beethoven's part.

The timpani motif is taken over by the clarinets and bassoons (b. 213), who eventually sustain an E major seventh chord while the soloist performs a long flourish of descending and ascending scale figures to lead to an orchestral ritornello, avoiding the expected cadence in A in favour of a sudden, brief tonal twist to F major (b. 224).

224–83 Ritornello 2

The full orchestra crashes in (F major) with the material first heard at b. 28, thus giving the 'development' significant impetus at an early stage. The ensuing bars appear on the surface to be little more than a repeat of bb. 28–88, but there are variants in the orchestration, accompanimental figuration and expressive annotations. Most of bb. 224–83 are *fortissimo* and the character of the second theme is transformed in a much more assertive version (b. 247); even the passage from b. 261 onwards, previously *piano* and *dolce* (at b. 166) is given a stronger identity. The tonality is all-important, too, Beethoven turning away from the tonic with a sudden harmonic twist and ending up in C major, a key utterly paradoxical to that of the concerto as a whole.

284–364 Second solo

As at b. 87, a sudden decrease in texture and dynamic ushers in the solo violin once more with a brief unaccompanied passage similar to its very first entry, this time in C major. Instead of re-introducing the expected first theme, it rests momentarily on a high $f \natural'''$ (b. 298), which is treated enharmonically (i.e. as an $e\sharp'''$) against the G in the cellos/basses, and the expected continuation in C major is subtly diverted on to the dominant of B minor. The timpani motif (basses) initiates a statement of the opening phrase of the first theme (in B minor), signalling in turn a long, episodic development of, principally, the material of bb. 2–5. This episodic quality of the development is a natural consequence of the contrast between solo and orchestra, for an ordinary symphonic development would tend to suppress the orchestra, to overwhelm the solo or to fall into crudely contrasted sections.[8] The bassoons have most of the thematic interest, incorporating especially the circular figure of b. 4, first in original and later in diminished note-values. The strings constantly remind us of the timpani figure, first in original and later in diminished note-values, while the soloist indulges in decorative figuration reminiscent of a Mozart piano concerto, moving down gradually through the dominants (B minor, E minor, A minor and D major) to achieve a very deliberate 'arrival' in the key of G minor (b. 331).

The horns quietly intone the timpani motif beneath the solo cadential trill and reiterate it while the soloist introduces a beautiful episode, featuring a new, poignant melody (b. 331). The bassoons take over the motif at b. 338 but pass it on to the trumpets and timpani, by which time the key of D minor is reached (b. 347) and the soloist's phrases become shorter and increasingly wistful above a falling chromatic passage of a quiet, meditative quality passing from tonic to dominant (bb. 351–7). This episode (bb. 331–57) provides both the emotional core of the movement and the point from which Beethoven finds his way back to the tonic key. Interestingly, soloists often reduce the tempo here, although no such change is indicated. Fiske believes that this tradition may be traceable to Joachim's performances,[9] but such deviation from a strict tempo was certainly part of the early-nineteenth-century aesthetic, Spohr recommending 'a slackening or lingering in those episodes expressive of tenderness and pathos' or an increase in tempo for fervent, impetuous passages.[10] Contemporary guidance from Czerny re the optimum tempo for the piano adaptation of this movement suggests ♩ = 126, but Kreisler adopted ♩ =112 and slowed to ♩ = 66 at b. 331, a more extreme change than the current norm of about ♩ = 80. The original tempo is usually re-established gradually during the soloist's ascending chromatic arpeggio passage over a pedal A (bb. 375ff.). The timpani motif reasserts itself in different parts of the orchestra and leads to a triumphant return of D major for the 'recapitulation'.

365–85 Ritornello 3

Beethoven's 'recapitulation' is strongly articulated, the structural significance of the landmark being accentuated by requiring the full orchestra to play, *fortissimo*, first the timpani motif and then a strident version of the first theme – quite a transformation from the serene mood of the opening!

In many small points of detail the ensuing bars are different from the original statement of the material; but there is no big surprise.

386–496 Third solo

The 'recapitulation' continues triumphantly with the transition theme (b. 382), taken up by the soloist (b. 386) and carried through new harmonic regions in preparation for a new scoring of the second idea (with phrases shared between clarinets/bassoons, oboes/horns/violas and solo violin). All is fairly regular until the extended dominant preparation yields an interrupted cadence instead of the expected perfect cadence in the tonic.

497–510 Ritornello 4 and solo cadenza

The orchestra again comes to the fore with the 'crashing' theme in a foreign key (once again B♭ major, b. 497), which in turn paves the way for a solo cadenza.

511–35 Coda

Beethoven requires the soloist to finish the cadenza quietly. The orchestra's re-entry after the concluding solo trill, comprising initially a pizzicato string accompaniment into which the woodwind gradually interpolate a more sustained line, is one of the most magical moments of all. Meanwhile, the soloist meditates for the first and only time over the lyrical second theme before engaging in a hushed duet with the first bassoon (b. 523). A terse crescendo, in which the cellos and then violas take up the bassoon's melody under energetic solo coloratura, brings the end.

Table 5.2 *The opening timpani motif and its various clearly defined recurrences in the first movement of Beethoven's Violin Concerto*

Bar nos.	Instrument	Comments	
		RITORNELLO 1 (TUTTI EXPOSITION)	
1–2	timp	tonic	♩ ♩ ♩ ♩ | ♩
4–5	obs, cls, bns		♩ ♩ ♩ ♩ | ♩
5–6	timp	dominant	♩ ♩ ♩ ♩ | ♩
8–9	timp (+ ob 2, cls, bns)	dominant-tonic	(♩)♩ ♩ ♩ | ♩
10–11	vns1	d♯ exposed, harmonic enigma	♪𝄾♪𝄾♪𝄾♪𝄾| 𝅝
11, 13–14	vcs, dbs		♪𝄾♪𝄾♪𝄾♪𝄾|(♩)
12–13	vns2, vas		♪𝄾♪𝄾♪𝄾♪𝄾| 𝅝
18, 20, 22	str	derived from b. 1	♫♫♫ ♫♫♫| ♪
28–35	orch	in modified forms:	♩ ♪𝄾♪𝄾 ♪ ♫♫♫ ♫♫♫ ♪𝄾♪𝄾| ♪
42–8	vns1	as accompaniment to	♩ ♩ ♩ ♫| ♩ ♩
49–50	obs, cls, bns	close of 2nd theme	♩ ♩ ♩ ♩ | ♩
50–6	hns, tpts, timp	accompanies 2nd theme (minore)	
57, 59	vns	extension of 2nd theme	
61, 63	obs, cls, bns, vns	extension of 2nd theme	
65–8	str	d♯ (b. 10) harmonised and so 'explained'	
73–4	vcs, dbs	in diminution	♫♫♫ ♪
87–9	bns, vcs/dbs, then vns, vas		♩ ♩ ♩ | 𝅝
		FIRST SOLO (SOLO EXPOSITION)	
101–2	timp	as bb. 1–2	
104–5	ob1, cls, bns	as bb. 4–5 + vn solo (decorated version)	
105–6	timp	as bb. 5–6	
108–9	obs, cls, bns	+ vn solo (decorated version)	
110–11	vns1	as bb. 10–11	
111, 113–14	vcs/dbs	as bb. 11, 13–14	
112–13	vns2 + vas	as bb. 12–13	
118, 120	str	as bb. 18, 20, 22	
122, 124, 126, 128, 130	timp, vcs/dbs		
150–1	vn solo	see bb. 49–50 (but in dominant)	

Table 5.2 (*cont.*)

Bar nos.	Instrument	Comments
158, 160	vns1, vas	see bb. 56, 58 (but in dominant minor)
162, 164	ob1, cl1, vns	see bb. 61, 63 (but in dominant minor)
166–9	vn solo, str	see bb. 65–8; d♯ now = a♯
172–3	str	motif in diminution ♩♩♩♩ ♩
201–2	vns, vas	motif in diminution ♪♩♩ ♩
206–11	vns, vcs/dbs, then str	
213–16	cls, bns	

RITORNELLO 2 (DEVELOPMENT)

Bar nos.	Instrument	Comments
224–31	orch (tpts and timp omitted at b. 226)	see bb. 28–35
238–45	vns1	
245	obs, cls, bns	similar to b. 49
246–7	fl, hns, tpts, vns, vas	♩ ♪ ♪ ♪
248–52	bns, hns, tpts	
253, 255, 257, 259	fl, obs,vns1	♩ ♩ ♩ ♩
261–4	fl, obs, bns, hns, tpts, vns1, vcs/dbs striking re-spelling of a♯′ to b♭′ in vns1 (also fl and bn1)	
268–9	vcs/dbs	motif in diminution ♩♩♩♩ ♩
282–4	vcs/dbs, then vns, vas	♩ ♩ ♩ ｜ 𝅝

SECOND SOLO

Bar nos.	Instrument	Comments
300–1	vcs/dbs	♪ ♪ ♪ ♪｜ 𝅝
303	vn solo, vns	
304–5	hns	♪ ♪ ♪ ♪｜ ♪
307–25	str, bns	legato ♩ ♩ ♩ ♩ ｜ ♩ and ♪ ♪ ♪ ♪｜ ♩ in alternation; rhythmic movement quickens to ♩♩♩♩ ♩ bb. 315 and is modified in bb. 319–20

Table 5.2 (*cont.*)

Bar nos.	Instrument	Comments	
330–7	hns	*pp* beneath solo episode (G minor)	♩ ♩ ♩ ♩ | 𝅝
338–45	bns	as hns at bb. 330–7	
346–57	tpts, timp from b. 350	as hns, bns bb. 330–45, but ♩♩♩♩|♩♩♩♩ etc.	
358–65	vn solo	rhythm of motto emphasised in triplet figuration, especially at bb. 361–5	
361	vns1	part of motif (pizz)	♪𝄾♪𝄾♪𝄾|
362	vns2	part of motif (pizz)	𝄾♪𝄾♪𝄾♪𝄾|
363	vas, vcs	part of motif (pizz)	𝄾♪𝄾♪𝄾♪𝄾|
364–5	obs, hns, timp	part of motif	𝄾♪𝄾♪𝄾♪𝄾| ♪𝄾

RITORNELLO 3 (RECAPITULATION)

Bar nos.	Instrument	Comments	
365–6, 368	orch	*ff* version of bb. 1ff.	♪𝄾♪𝄾♪𝄾♪𝄾|
369–70	hns, tpts, timp, str		♪𝄾♪𝄾♪𝄾♪𝄾| 𝅝
372–3	hns, tpts, timp, vcs/dbs		
374–5	vns, vas	d♯' now *forte*	♪𝄾♪𝄾♪𝄾♪𝄾| 𝅝
375	hns, tpts, timp, vcs, dbs		♪𝄾♪𝄾♪𝄾♪𝄾|
376	bns, vns2, vas		
377	hns, tpts, timp, vas, vcs/dbs		
382, 384	timp, vcs/dbs		♬♬ ♬♬| ♪

THIRD SOLO

Bar nos.	Instrument	Comments	
386, 388, 390	str		♬♬ ♬♬| ♪
392–4	str, vn solo		
396–8	ob1, cls, str, vn solo (decorated version)		
400, 402	str		♬♬ ♬♬| ♪
404	vns, vas		♬♬ ♬♬| ♪
424	vn solo		
432, 434	vns		

Table 5.2 (*cont.*)

Bar nos.	Instrument	Comments
436, 438	fl, ob1, vns	
440–4	vn solo, vns, vas, vcs	
446–7	str	♩♪♪♪♩
480–1	vns1, vcs/dbs	
482–3	vns1	
484–5	str	
487–90	obs, hns	
		RITORNELLO 4
497–504	orch	modified (as bb. 28–35)
509–10	fl, obs, cls, hns, tpts, timp	
		CODA (CODA)
517	vn solo	
518–19	obs, hns	
520–1	hns	
521–3	vn solo	in augmentation

6

Structure and style II – 2/3. Larghetto – Rondo: Allegro

Reviews of Beethoven's works roughly contemporaneous with the Violin Concerto, such as the Third Piano Concerto and the 'Eroica' Symphony, have in common a concern for unity of structure within movements.[1] As its first movement clearly demonstrates, Beethoven's Violin Concerto also responds to such concerns for integration and coherence, and some commentators have even perceived an inner motivic unity within the piece as a whole. Yehudi Menuhin, for example, connects the last three notes of the first oboe part in 1/4 with the first three notes of the scale melody introduced by clarinets and bassoons at 1/18, the first three notes (first violins) of the Larghetto, and the last three notes of the first phrase of the principal theme of the finale (solo violin, b. 4), claiming that his observation provides 'just one small clue to three notes which otherwise, deprived of their symbolic value, would be just three notes of the ascending scale'.[2] He also suggests a relationship between the melodic line of bb. 3 and 4 of the Larghetto and the opening theme of the first movement and particularly the soloist's minor-mode re-statement of this melody at 1/301. While the prominent scale/arpeggio characteristics of much of the first movement's material lend themselves to such analysis in connection with, for example, the solo violin part in 2/51,[3] Menuhin is straining credibility in claiming something other than a mere arpeggio relationship between the explosive tutti figure at 1/28 and the soloist's first elaboration of the theme in the Larghetto (b. 11) or the opening theme of the finale. And it is surely misleading to link the soloist's G minor episode in the first movement (b. 331) with the Larghetto's melodic material at bb. 65 and 79!

Larghetto[4]

The simple, serene Larghetto clearly has its roots in variation form, but most commentators have been at a loss to describe it accurately in terms of traditional structures. Tovey boldly states, 'the form is that of a theme and variations' in which he discerns 'sublime inaction' and a parallel with the corresponding movements of the 'Appassionata' Sonata (Op. 57) and the 'Archduke' Trio (Op. 97); Roger Fiske, however, describes it as one of Beethoven's 'semi-variation movements' with virtually no attempt at contrast of mood or key, while Hans Joachim Moser, acknowledging that the thematic material is 'variiert ', calls the basic ten-bar phrase a 'Ritornell-Thema', which forms a 'Strophe' that is repeated four times in a songlike manner.[5] By contrast, George Grove makes no mention of variation, and Basil Deane focuses more on the process of repetition than variation. Deane observes that the movement 'consists of five statements of a ten-bar phrase in G major, interlinked with another phrase contributed by the soloist' and isolates orchestral colour and the 'ethereal embroidery of the solo violin' as its other significant characteristics. Other scholars concentrate more on the movement's 'unchanging tonality'; its static harmonic plan follows the precedent of the Triple Concerto, remaining largely in the tonic key of G major (apart from the very end, which incorporates dominant preparation for the finale) and allowing the material to unfold freely.[6] In the final analysis the Larghetto comprises not so much variations as varied orchestrations of Theme A (first violins, bb. 1–10), this melody recurring almost throughout virtually unaltered apart from its scoring. Table 6.1 provides an outline of its unconventional, open-ended structure alongside Owen Jander's descriptors, which are discussed later.

Table 6.1 Structural outline of the second movement: Larghetto

Bar Nos.	Content	Jander's description
1–10	Theme A	Strophe I
11–20	Variation 1 of Theme A	Strophe II
21–30	Variation 2 of Theme A	Strophe III
31–40	Variation 3 of Theme A	Strophe IV
40³–4	Ornamental extension	Interruption of the *Romanze*

Table 6.1 (*cont.*)

Bar Nos.	Content	Jander's description
45–55	Theme B	
56–65	Variation 4 of Theme A	Strophe V
65–70	Theme C	
71–9	Reprise of Theme B (elaborated)	Dispute in dialogue resolved
79–83	Reprise of Theme C	
83–8		Coda
83–91	Coda (using Theme A and ending on V of D major)	
88–91		Conclusion of sublime experience

Theme A (bb. 1–10)

Theme A, with its rich 'local' modulations and its pregnant silences (reminiscent of the slow movement of the Piano Sonata in E♭ major Op. 7), is announced by muted orchestral violins with string accompaniment. Of ten bars' length, its phrase structure is distributed in a format of 4 (or possibly 1+1+2) bars + 6 (or possibly 4+2) bars, the main division marked by a prolonged dominant chord of B minor (which becomes a pause in variations 1 and 2).

Variation 1 of Theme A (bb. 10–20)

The theme is taken up by the horns and (one bar later) the first clarinet supported by the upper strings. The soloist's role is decorative, adding a descant, largely in semiquaver scale or arpeggio figuration. Bars 8 and 9 of the theme are sometimes earmarked, though not always convincingly, as the possible derivation of the soloist's ornamental figuration. The end of the first phrase (b. 14) is punctuated by a pause and a brief written-out *ad libitum* passage for the soloist.

Variation 2 of Theme A (bb. 21–30)

The first bassoon has the melody on this occasion, supported by violas (at times divided) and cellos with pizzicato violin and bass punctuation. The soloist's embroidery is more complex (largely sextuplets and demisemiquavers), yet it shadows the theme more closely. It becomes increasingly florid during the course of the crescendoing second phrase, which is set off from the first by a pause on a trill and a somewhat different *ad libitum* ornamental termination.

Variation 3 of Theme A (bb. 31–40)

The solo decorations build to a climax at b. 30 to introduce a reprise of Theme A by the full orchestra. Without pause for breath at the end of the first phrase, the first violins sing the melody in full voice, supported by the other members of their family. The wind instruments largely echo the rhythm of the opening three notes of the melody, but the first clarinet and first bassoon eventually join with the first violins in intoning the theme's final two bars.

Ornamental extension (bb. 40³–4)

With the minimum of orchestral participation, the soloist introduces some free *dolce* arabesques as a kind of tonic prolongation, rising to *d'''* and then descending, via various off-beat notes of emphasis and an eventual diminuendo, to take up the role of melodist for the first time in the movement.

Theme B (bb. 45–55)

The soloist's new melody (Theme B), introduced on the two lower strings (in contrast with the previous ornamental filigree) over the quietest and most slow-moving of string accompaniments, has been shown to have affiliations with Theme A (Ex. 6.1).[7] The tonality remains firmly in G major but the mood here is even more still and serene. Theme B is essentially an eight-bar melody whose cadential trill is repeated an octave higher; typically, it introduces a scale passage, first ascending and then descending, which links into the subsequent section.

Variation 4 of Theme A (bb. 56–65)

The violins pluck the outline of Theme A over a simple pizzicato string accompaniment (without basses) which provides the momentum for this

6.1 Beethoven: Violin Concerto in D major Op. 61 (2nd movement),
illustrating the elements in common between Themes A and B

variation. The soloist contributes appropriate *cantabile* embroidery
above, sometimes shadowing the orchestral violins with a syncopated
version of the theme.

Theme C (bb. 65–70)

The last bar of the fourth variation introduces a new idea (Theme C),
related to Theme A only by the horns' rhythmic figure (bb. 65–7), which
is reminiscent of A's opening three notes. A brief *crescendo* is followed by
a sudden *piano*, at which point the soloist provides a link into the reprise
of Theme B.

Reprise of Theme B (elaborated) (bb. 71–9)

The soloist recalls Theme B in an embellished form, a sparse, slow-
moving *pianissimo* woodwind accompaniment replacing the shimmering
string foundation of its previous appearance.

Reprise of Theme C (bb. 79–83)

Theme C returns in modified and shortened form. A more expansive
solo *roulade* (b. 81) and an additional statement of the prominent dotted
rhythmic figure in the horns inspire the soloist in new directions
appropriate to the movement's coda.

Coda (bb. 83–91)

The opening bars of the coda, based firmly in G major, comprise essentially decorated solo versions of the tonic chord, punctuated by the

orchestral strings. As the soloist rises to the higher registers, the accompaniment lightens and the solo contribution diminishes to a whisper.[8] The soloist reminisces peacefully over the figuration of the first variation while the muted horns, and then muted violins, quietly announce the opening motif of Theme A. The scene is set for one of Beethoven's most dramatic gestures. With violins now unmuted, the orchestral strings are suddenly unleashed in full voice. The dotted rhythmic motif of A is transformed into a double-dotted figure which propels the music powerfully through a brusque conventional modulation, concluding on the dominant of D major. The subsequent cadenza leads straight into the finale, normally by way of Beethoven's brief written-out link.

Some musicologists have sought an historically credible method of accounting for the structural idiosyncrasies of the movement, for it is so unlike the traditional variation types of the period, such as those based on themes in binary form, or on opera airs or popular tunes, that it has proved difficult to describe accurately in conventional terms. Owen Jander has offered one of the most persuasive and authoritative accounts of this movement in recent times, perceptively ascribing its individual character to three factors: the influence of the contemporaneous *Romanze*; the presence of a chaconne bass within the structure; and the poetic and subjective qualities added by the quasi-programmatic dialogue between soloist and orchestra.[9]

In Beethoven's time, the popularity of the *Romanze* as a genre in Western poetry was often reflected in musical terms, especially in the slow movements of late-eighteenth- and early-nineteenth-century concertos. Koch observes that it was becoming preferred to the aria-like ABA′ slow movement. He quotes Sulzer:

'Nowadays one gives the name *Romanze* to little narrative songs in the extremely naïve and rather antique tone of the old rhymed Romances. The content of these songs is a narrative of passionate, tragic, sentimental or merry content. [Koch's note: In instrumental compositions one does not make use of the *Romanze* in this last-named sense, since such movements will always employ a slow tempo]. The theme and the expression must be of utmost simplicity, and naïve in the extreme. Such a composition is usually clothed in the form of a rondo...'[10]

Koch's last statement is borne out by modern scholars, Roger Hickman, for example, confirming that the simplicity, lyricism and form of the vocal *romance* were easily adapted by composers of instrumental music. 'In the 18th century', Hickman continues, 'the term was frequently applied to slow movements with a rondo, ABA or variation structure which featured a simple binary theme.'[11] However, as Jander warns, it would be misleading to describe the *Romanze* primarily as a form; 'it is a genre, which in both its poetic and musical manifestations can assume a variety of forms', as is evident from J. J. Rousseau's definition (*Dictionnaire de Musique*, Paris, 1768), later cited in German translation by Sulzer:

> An air to which one sings a little poem of the same name, divided into strophes [*couplets*], the subject of which is ordinarily some amorous, and often tragic, story. Since the romance should be written in a style that is simple, affecting, and in a somewhat antique taste [*d'un goût un peu antique*], the air should respond to the character of the words: not at all ornamented [*point d'ornemens*], devoid of mannerisms, a melody that is sweet, natural and pastoral [*champêtre*], and which produces its effect all by itself, independent of the manner of the singer. It is not necessary that the song be lively; it suffices that it be naïve, and that it in no way obscure the text, which it should allow to be clearly heard, and that it not employ a large vocal range. A well-made *romance*, having nothing striking about it, does not move one right at the outset. But each strophe adds something to the effect of the preceding ones, and the interest grows imperceptibly; and the listener finds himself moved to tears without being able to say where the charm lies that has produced this effect.[12]

Jander claims that Beethoven's Larghetto is faithful to Rousseau's definition of the romance in five respects: in its use of an essentially strophic form; in its pastoral atmosphere; in various musical details that suggest the 'goût un peu antique '; in its quasi-narrative character; and in 'its touching and extremely Romantic final experience'. He considers particularly apt Moser's use of the term 'strophes' in his analytical description; as the movement proceeds from strophe to strophe, the melody is passed unaltered from orchestral instrument to instrument (strings, horn, clarinet, bassoon, strings) in keeping with Rousseau's specification 'point d'ornemens.' The movement's pastoral atmosphere, conveyed jointly by its overall serenity, lyricism, slow harmonic rhythm,

6.2 Beethoven: Violin Concerto in D major Op. 61 (2nd movement), showing the chaconne bass-line and its derivation

soft dynamic and transparency of orchestration, in which the pastoral character of the horns is especially prominent, offers a further link with Rousseau's description (his use of the word 'champêtre'). And Jander is adamant that Rousseau's prerequisite for the genre of a style 'd'un goût un peu antique' is satisfied admirably by the chaconne element of Beethoven's movement, for 'The "theme"...has a bass line that uses the venerable four-note tetrachord, plus the conventional four-note consequent' (Ex. 6.2).

Beethoven used the tetrachordal bass pattern, in variant form, in three other movements more or less contemporary with his Violin Concerto: the first and slow movements of the 'Waldstein' Sonata Op. 53

(1803–4), and the Thirty-two Variations on an Original Theme (WoO80, 1806). However, its treatment in this Larghetto is unorthodox, Jander distinguishing the following departures from the traditional historical pattern:

1. The theme is ten bars long.
2. The descent from pitch 8 to pitch 7 is delayed until the last beat of the third bar.
3. Pitches 6 and 5 arrive on the second beats of the bar (in bb. 5 and 6).
4. The dominant, once reached, is drawn out for two bars (bb. 6 and 7).
5. *The dominant is then resolved* – and in the middle of the pattern (N.B. the middle of the pattern occurs at b. 8 in this ten-bar theme).
6. The first and second spans of the pattern (called respectively the 'arsis' and 'thesis') are extremely asymmetrical in length, the arsis taking up eight bars, the thesis two (as in WoO80).
7. In the unfolding of the movement, arsis and thesis are separated from one another, each being used (or suggested) without the other: the thesis, alone, in bb. 49–56 and 75–9, and the arsis alluded to, abortively, at the end of the movement.
8. The pattern is set aside at a couple of places, but its disappearance and recurrence serve as important events in the total form.
9. The metre is not the conventional triple (3/2 or 3/4), but 4/4.
10. The tempo, *larghetto*, is far slower than any tetrachordal pieces in the Baroque tradition, resulting in a harmonic rhythm so protracted that it disguises the chaconne identity of the movement.

Of course, other earlier works have deviated from the norm in many of the above ways, notably in the use of something other than an eight-bar pattern; but the more usual approach involved the compression rather than the protraction of this pattern exemplified in Beethoven's Larghetto. Beethoven's approach may also be considered individualistic in its stretching of the dominant in bb. 6 and 7, and its resolution of that dominant in b. 8. Jander considers this resolution of the dominant at the end of the tetrachordal descent (the arsis), prior to the thesis, as being 'utterly antithetical.'[13] The overall harmonic feeling that always accompanied music written over tetrachordal basses required a nonresolution of that dominant that occurs midway (or roughly midway) in such patterns, but Beethoven's unconventional (antithetical) resolution of the

6.3 Beethoven: Violin Concerto in D major Op. 61 (2nd movement), comparing Beethoven's arsis–thesis relationship with tradition

6.4 Beethoven: Violin Concerto in D major Op. 61 (2nd movement), comparing Beethoven's treatment of the harmonic accents of the thesis with tradition

dominant in b. 8 of his theme fundamentally alters the harmonic phrase-ology that is traditional to such tetrachordal bass patterns, upsetting the original arsis–thesis feeling and making the 'thesis' assume the effect of an 'afterthought.' This becomes all the stronger as a result of the arsis–thesis relationship already created in bb. 1–4 and 5–8 (Ex. 6.3). Jander further observes that Beethoven sheds the traditional feeling of the tetrachordal formula by what he does with the harmonic accents of the four pitches of the thesis, 3–4–5–1. Traditionally, these four har-monies are rhythmically strong–weak–strong–weak; but Beethoven reverses these rhythmic accents in bb. 8–10 (Ex. 6.4).

Traditionally, most chaconnes or passacaglias have a continuous quality, largely because each statement of the bass pattern ends either on the dominant or with a 'feminine' cadence. Beethoven, however, ends his version of the pattern in an extremely conclusive, 'masculine' manner,

83

6.5 Beethoven: Violin Concerto in D major Op. 61 (2nd movement), the triple
metre/sarabande implications

presumably, as Jander suggests, to stress the effect of each 'variation'
being, in fact, a strophe. His preference for 4/4 instead of triple metre
(3/2 or 3/4) represents another significant departure from convention,
as tetrachordal basses are historically linked to the chaconne and pas-
sacaglia, both of which are dances in triple metre. Yet this metre is often
disguised by Beethoven's placement of the dominant-to-tonic progres-
sions on beats 1 and 2 of bb. 1, 2, 5 and 6, with the result that the harmonic weight is given to the normally weak second beats of the bar. At
the same time, the third beats of those bars, normally points of rhythmic
strength, are given over to rests, thus implying triple metre. As Jander
writes, 'It is almost as though he [Beethoven] had created here a slow-
paced, dreamy sarabande, in which the prolongation of the second beat,
so characteristic of that dance, is made mysterious through silence' (Ex.
6.5).[14] Jander further points out the long association in history between
the chaconne and the rhythm of the sarabande and he is convinced that
Beethoven was aware of that association, citing as evidence the composer's ponderous use of the sarabande rhythm in the C minor Variations WoO80.

Jander has focused much of his work on the vogue for musical dialogue in the late eighteenth and early nineteenth centuries, as well as on

Beethoven's fascination with musical rhetoric in general, and musical dialogue in particular.[15] He relates the quasi-narrative character of Beethoven's Larghetto to Rousseau's claim that the vocal romance should recite an 'amorous and often tragic story', and he attempts to divine Beethoven's poetic intentions, interpreting the slow movement subjectively as a dialogue between the orchestra and soloist; as in the slow movement of the Fourth Piano Concerto, the customary roles are reversed, with the orchestra, not the soloist, acting as the singer of the song. His commentary on how the programmatic dialogue unfolds, though made with reference to contemporary treatises, is arguably of questionable content, but his analysis of the movement's various subdivisions (presented in Table 6.1) is beyond dispute.

As in the 'Romanze' of Beethoven's Second Piano Concerto Op. 19, the succession of strophes builds to a climax towards the middle of the movement (in this case after Strophe IV), the remainder becoming, in both cases, 'a meditative aftermath to that climax'. Jander also relates the delicate pizzicato accompaniment of Strophe V (bb. 56–65) to Rousseau's view that a romance should be provided only with the most sparing accompaniment and may be most effective with no accompaniment at all. Sulzer is noncommittal as to the truth of Rousseau's assertion, but his claim that romances accompanied by a mandolin produced for him the desired effect suggests that Beethoven's use of pizzicato strings may, indeed, have some significance. Jander describes the function of the coda as 'resolution through the experience of transfiguration'.[16] Although fairly new in 1806, the concept of transfiguration (*Verklärung*) was anticipated in philosophical and aesthetic debates of the late eighteenth century; with the distinction between the beautiful and the sublime as the principal recurrent topic, transfiguration was to become ubiquitous in Romantic literature and music in the following decades of the nineteenth century.

For a composer whose ambition, by his own admission, was to be known as a 'tone-poet', Beethoven seems naturally to have been drawn to the idea of the romance as an instrumental genre, employing the form in three single-movement works: the Romanze Cantabile for piano, flute, bassoon and orchestra, and the two Romances for violin and orchestra Opp. 40 and 50. His poetic intentions thus provide the clues to his unorthodox and individualistic treatment of the slow movement of his

Violin Concerto. To describe it simply as a theme and variations would ignore the philosophical and aesthetic debates of late-eighteenth-century musicians and theorists and underestimate the extent of Beethoven's extra-musical inspiration.

Finale: Rondo: Allegro[17]

As in Beethoven's Triple Concerto and Fourth and Fifth Piano Concertos, the slow movement is linked to the finale. Such interconnection has precedents in piano concertos by, for example, Kozeluch, Dussek and Woelfl, all composed before 1800, and became a common practice of the period in many instrumental genres, bringing the moods of the two movements into a closer relationship and setting the moment of transition to the finale into sharp relief.[18] Beethoven retains the style of the light-hearted, eighteenth-century rondo finale and modifies it to suit his purpose. He introduces greater contrast and an increased level of tension by placing the second episode in a minor key (G minor), an admirable counterbalance to the major–minor ambiguity of the first movement, whose development adopts a similar tonal bias. It is a 'hunting' rondo of standard design with substantial coda, dividing conveniently into seven main sections: A1–B1–A2–C1–A3–B2–Coda (A4).

Section A1 (bb. 1–58)

The soloist at once introduces the rondo refrain, of which an old Viennese tradition names Clement as the creator.[19] It is a lively, light-hearted tune of dance-like character played on the G string, initially to a light, somewhat sparse cello accompaniment. After an enquiring one-bar solo appendage, encouraged by fuller orchestration, and an orchestral reply, most prominently by the oboes and horns, who then seem to pause to catch their breath, the refrain is repeated *delicatamente* two octaves higher by the soloist, this time with discreet accompaniment from the orchestral violins. A similar two-bar passage of solo questioning and orchestral comment, ending on a pause, leads to a *fortissimo* statement of the refrain by the full orchestra, at the end of which its last four notes are extended upwards by the interval of a third to introduce a new idea (b. 31). This strongly accented figure, characterised by its prominent dotted rhythm, links into the next solo passage, the music gradually quietening down as the strings of the orchestra repeat their tonic/dominant motivic pattern (bb. 41–4). The soloist takes up this pattern and throws it aloft while the horns contribute a characteristic hunting fanfare, which, richly elaborated by the soloist and taken up by other departments of the orchestra, modulates to the dominant and serves as a neat transition to the next section.

Section B1 (bb. 58–92)

Veering between the dominant major and minor, the main motif of B1 is presented by the full orchestra and answered by the soloist in the manner of a dialogue. The soloist then embarks on some challenging passage-work, while the first bassoon has a prominent role to play in the light orchestral texture. However, it is not long before first the violas, then the first violins, the cellos and basses and eventually the first oboe and first bassoon remind us in turn, and with increasing insistence, of the principal rondo idea. A pause on the dominant, decorated by the soloist with a trill and written-out termination, brings B1 to a close.

Section A2 (bb. 92–127)

Bars 92–116 of this section are identical in content and presentation to bb. 1–24 inclusive. The second part of the full orchestral statement of the theme, however, holds some tonal surprises, replacing the tonic major chord with one of the tonic minor (b. 117) and developing the main motif of the rondo theme in dialogue fashion through an ingenious series of modulations occasioned by an ascending chromatic bass-line. The soloist takes over at the height of the orchestral conversation and prepares for the very different mood of section C1.

Section C1 (bb. 127–73)

The second episode of this rondo structure is based in the subdominant (G) minor. The soloist, accompanied by sustained strings, introduces the first eight bars of a sweet, soulful melody, which is repeated, over a lighter string background, by a solo bassoon with additional violin solo filigree. The second half of the melody, with its initial limb in the relative major (Bb), is similarly presented, first by the violin soloist and then by the bassoon, with violin solo elaboration. The soloist marks time for a few bars (bb. 158–61) while the strings effect a move towards D minor in preparation for the oboes and orchestral violins (both groups in thirds) to take up the second half of this melody once more, again adorned with solo violin filigree but quietening gradually to a whisper. This is the cue for the re-entry of the rondo motif (strings), imitated in more complex octave figuration by the soloist. Such imitation continues through a chromatic ascent by the bar (bb. 169–72) until the dominant seventh chord of D major launches the soloist into two climactic bars of octave passagework, begging the return of the rondo theme.

Section A3 (bb. 173–233)

Bars 174–217 are the same as bb. 1–44 and bb. 218–21 are in most respects similar to bb. 45–8, apart from the fact that this time the soloist enters pizzicato (and an octave lower) and plays the subsequent phrase an octave lower than before.

Section B2 (bb. 233–79)

The content of much of this section is very similar to bb. 58–92, the major–minor conflict this time centring on the tonic. Over violin solo passagework very similar to Section B1, but with a different tonal bias, the main rondo motif starts reappearing in the cellos at b. 255, answered initially by the first violins. It later progresses in modified form through the woodwind, initially in alternation with the cellos and basses, in the order flute, first bassoon, first oboe, first bassoon and first clarinet. After a two-bar diminuendo, the soloist arrives at a trill on the dominant; under this the fanfare first heard at b. 46, commencing *pianissimo* (horns and oboes initially) but crescendoing all the time, grows to a full orchestral tutti with first the clarinets, bassoons, second violins, violas and cellos (b. 273) and later the flute, trumpets, timpani and first violins and double basses (b. 275) joining in the fray. A two-bar cadential phrase leads to the conventional fermata on the chord of the tonic six-four in preparation for the solo cadenza.

Coda A4 (bb. 280–360)

After the solo cadenza there is an unusually long coda, occasioned largely by the surprising modulation to the remote key of A♭, which requires a long and complex harmonic progression for a satisfactory return to the tonic. Under an extended trill from the soloist, cellos and basses enter with pertinent references to the principal theme. Receiving no recognition from the soloist, they give way to the violins; faltering somewhat, they are met half way by the soloist, who changes his trill note from d'' to $e♭''$. Two bars later (b. 293) the dance resumes (in A♭ major) with a modified version of the rondo refrain, and it is only through a remarkable sequence of harmonies that the main rondo idea, in embellished form (solo violin), works its way back to the tonic from arguably the furthest possible point of departure. After a trill on the dominant, the soloist has four bars of unaccompanied *pianissimo* to forge the final links in the chain (a resemblance may be noted between 3/311–14 and 2/3). A delightful dialogue on the rondo theme then ensues between the first oboe and the soloist; the first violins join in and soon provide the necessary support to the soloist's arabesques to create a glorious final climax. With the rondo motif in evidence at fairly regular intervals in the bass instruments, the solo violin shows its supremacy over the whole orchestra by peppering its pertinent outbursts with arpeggios and scales. The mood becomes more unruly with the orchestral syncopations at bb. 341–2 and 345–6 but the soloist's *fortissimo* arpeggio and piano scale formula keep the orchestra in check. The final twelve bars are based almost entirely on a D major triad, the orchestra attempting to contribute one last statement of the refrain but without complete success. Instead, it is the soloist who takes advantage of the orchestra's sudden diminuendo by offering a last quiet unaccompanied version of the dance-like theme. Two crashing tutti chords provide the final perfect cadence.

7

Cadenzas

The Classical and early Romantic eras witnessed a gradual expansion in the scope of the cadenza, which tended to adopt a more significant structural role by incorporating relevant thematic material from the movement rather than comprising mere cadential elaboration. In the first movement in particular, the cadenza fulfilled both an architectural function, with its climactic passage for the soloist balancing the orchestral ritornello, and a dramatic one of allowing the soloist free rein for unfettered solo display. Originally improvisations or passages intended to sound like improvisations, some cadenzas were actually written out by composers either for use in performance or as models for students to imitate. Most of the authentic cadenzas by Mozart for his piano concertos and, to a certain extent, the written-out cadenza in his Sinfonia Concertante K.364 serve as excellent models of the Classical cadenza. Although their content is varied and imaginative, the majority of Mozart's surviving piano concerto cadenzas (with the exception of some second- and third-movement examples) typically adopt a tripartite design, bound together, as it were, in one harmonic progression. The first (and largest) subdivision normally commenced either with one of the principal themes of the movement (e.g. K.453, first movement), with the figure heard during the cadential preparation, or with an energetic virtuoso flourish, which may also have thematic affinities (e.g. K.271 first movement), emanating from the harmonic tension of the initial tonic six-four chord. This is followed by a more reflective section, comprising a thematic statement in the tonic, usually of a cantabile second subject. This latter is not normally presented in its entirety, but is fragmented and extended sequentially (or it may be presented more fully with new harmonies), passing through but rarely establishing a variety of close keys. A descent to a sustained chord or long note in the lower register eventually serves as a point of departure for further technical display, incorporating scales, arpeggios and suchlike, prior to the brief, normally non-thematic closing transition to the final cadential trill on the dominant seventh chord.[1]

The early nineteenth century witnessed further changes. Beethoven preserved the tradition of cadenza improvisation in his first four piano concertos and his Violin Concerto, but he often wrote down some ideas before performances, as various cadenza sketches from the 1790s clearly indicate.[2] However, his desire to exert greater control over this part of the concerto is evident in his explicit instructions to the performer (e.g. 'La Cadenza sia corta' or 'let the cadenza be short' in the third movement of Op. 58), his integration of cadenza-equivalent passages into the solo part of his Fifth Piano Concerto Op. 73 ('The Emperor'), and his subsequent compliance with the increasing trend of composing cadenzas for concerted works. In c1809, he provided cadenzas for each of his first four piano concertos and his piano version of Op. 61; in fact three alternative cadenzas are known for both the First Piano Concerto and the first movement of the Fourth. Each was composed after the relevant concerto had been published, but none of the cadenzas was printed during his lifetime.

The relation of Beethoven's cadenzas to the movements for which they were intended varies, as does their character, some comprising merely virtuosic pianistic figurations and others incorporating real thematic developments. Unlike Mozart's cadenzas, no consistent skeletal outline for Beethoven's can be distinguished, although he begins with an imitative working out of the head motif of the principal theme in over half his cadenzas. Furthermore, his harmonic and tonal vocabulary is generally wider and his cadenzas vary substantially in length from the miniature 5-bar passage labelled 'cadenza' in the rondo of his Fourth Piano Concerto to the enormous 125- and 126-bar cadenzas for the first movements of his First Piano Concerto and the piano adaptation of his Violin Concerto.

Beethoven allows opportunity for a cadenza in each of the three movements of his Violin Concerto. Interestingly, only two of his piano concertos (Opp. 15 and 58) and his Violin Concerto provide the opportunity for a cadenza in the finale. If reports of his concerto and other performances are accurate, Clement would have relished the opportunity to display his prodigious technical skills in some lengthy cadenzas, possibly with somewhat dubious artistic goals in mind. In a performance of a Rode concerto in January, 1805, one reviewer rebuked him for extending the fantasy element too long and thereby interrupting the continuity of the movement.[3]

Beethoven's somewhat ambivalent attitude to the cadenza is illustrated by the fact that he provided no cadenzas for his Violin Concerto, but wrote four for his piano adaptation of that work. That for the first movement is one of Beethoven's longest cadenzas and it is particularly remarkable for its use of timpani during the Marcia section (bb. 36–54) and thereafter. This 'intrusive little four-square quick march', as Tovey calls it, may be 'a topical allusion to *Fidelio*'.[4] Especially striking are its regular phrasing and its exploitation of the very motif which permeates the movement. Whitmore describes it as 'a remarkably trite passage', because 'it serves as a relief to the intensity of the surrounding improvisatory passages, in the way that lyrical secondary themes in cadenzas normally do, but the (deliberate) effect here is not so much of relaxation as of bathos'.[5] The cadenza's opening comprises a literal quotation of the first eight bars of the preceding tutti (which are in turn a transposition of bb. 28–35); such repetition of material, coupled with some unpianistic writing and the shock of the B♭ major harmony immediately following the cadential fermata makes one question the cadenza's success; but its climax is well calculated, the material of the first thirteen bars of the movement returning as thick piano chords. The virtuosic continuation leads directly to the final trill, under which the pianist and timpanist join in an emphatic reference to that ubiquitous timpani motive.

Beethoven also composed a fresh link between the second and third movements and a modest, apposite finale cadenza characterised by its constant momentum. Semiquaver figuration is maintained throughout, whether as neutral bravura passagework or allusion to bb. 273–6 from the cadential preparation (themselves derived from bb. 46–7), but the consistent quasi-orchestral textures result in piano writing which is far from idiomatic. The proper location for the third of Beethoven's cadenzas for Op. 61a is questionable. It does not fit comfortably at 3/278, incorporating no pertinent thematic material and merely treating a simple figure sequentially in various rhythmic patterns. Bar 92 seems the most likely place for its insertion, the simple figure elaborated in the cadenza then acting as a development of the notated *Nachschlag* which closes the solo trill. Because of the absence of any original cadenzas for the Violin Concerto, violinists' searches for authentic material and the novelty value of introducing an 'accompanied' cadenza have prompted some to adapt for the violin Beethoven's piano cadenzas for Op. 61a. Those who have pursued this course include Ottakar Novácek, Max Rostal, Michelangelo Abbado, Wolfgang Schneiderhan, Joseph Swensen and, to some extent, Joseph Hellmesberger Sen. Hellmesberger made a partial transcription and adaptation of Beethoven's first-movement cadenza, combining large amounts of Beethoven's material both from the cadenza and from the first movement with some of his own and requiring orchestral participation virtually throughout. Novácek's and Schneiderhan's more effective transcriptions achieve a closer approximation to Beethoven's originals, preserving as much as possible the cadenzas' thematic content and adapting the technical requirements to the different character of the instrument. Kremer's controversial adaptation of Beethoven also introduces a piano, positioned off-stage and transmitted to the orchestra through loudspeakers. Although these adaptations offer some gratifying moments and provide a valuable opportunity to comprehend Beethoven's objectives, even if intended for a different instrument, they do not translate well to the violin. Furthermore, like the modern custom of playing cadenzas by Mozart and Beethoven whenever they exist, they introduce a wholly foreign element of fixity into a convention that was intended to encourage a wide range of expression.

More cadenzas have been published for this than for any other violin concerto.[6] Apart from those based on Beethoven's own cadenzas for Op. 61a, they provide an illuminating insight into the differing musical and performing styles of their particular times. One of the few sets of published cadenzas by a contemporary of the composer were those of Louis Spohr, despite Spohr's stated dislike of the piece. That for the first movement is of Classical spirit, comprising essentially a cadential elaboration of tripartite design. Apart from reference to the soloist's first entry and some vague associations with the timpani motif at the end, its nineteen bars are essentially non-thematic, its middle section incorporating sequential development with some surprising harmonic twists. Spohr's second-movement cadenza dispenses with Beethoven's prescribed ending and is essentially an elaborate non-thematic linking passage, although it does recall 1/87–8 and anticipate the finale's main rondo theme. His cadenza for the finale also has little direct thematic association with its parent movement, comprising largely tasteful 'improvisation' and incorporating some awkward double stopping in tenths.

Appropriately enough, the cadenzas by the concerto's greatest champions, Joachim and Kreisler, are the most often played. Of Joachim's two sets of cadenzas, the second is somewhat easier and more accessible but the first has provided the challenge for most converts to Joachim's work. Its seventy-six-bar, first-movement cadenza admirably combines extempore qualities with pertinent thematic material and sustains the predominantly lyrical character of the movement. The timpani motif and, to a lesser extent, the dramatic gestures of 1/28 and the solo entry dominate the first section (bb. 1–40); then follows an effective, *con delicatezza* development of the timpani motif, mostly in left-hand pizzicato, and the second theme in the triplet rhythm of the soloist's accompaniment at 1/41–51. Much of the rest of the cadenza is built around the soloist's entry at 1/89 and its related passagework. A *fortissimo* descending chromatic scale in octaves (bb. 63–4) heralds a dramatic return of the timpani motif (bb. 65–9 and 74–6), which, together with further reminiscences of passagework from the First Solo (bb. 71–4), leads into Beethoven's coda. The first set's cadenza for the Larghetto incorporates Beethoven's prescribed six-note lead-in early on, but continues by developing Theme C (2/65–70) before proceeding to a trill on the dominant and a chromatic ascent to the rondo theme's anacrusis. Joachim's favoured cadenza for the finale comprises largely an elaboration of the principal theme but also incorporates some skilful two-part counterpoint.

Kreisler's cadenzas, composed in 1894, sum up 'the essence of Beethoven's music as a few drops of attar of rose do the fragrance of an acre of flowers'.[7] This is especially true of his first-movement cadenza (sixty-six bars), even if its ingenious climax (b. 45), when the two principal themes are triumphantly combined in counterpoint, may seem artificially contrived. Critics have not been so effusive about Kreisler's cadenza for the Larghetto, disliking in particular its anticipation of the 6/8 metre and main thematic substance of the ensuing rondo.[8] His fifty-two-bar cadenza for the finale is often abridged in performance, some of its superfluous passagework being omitted in order to emphasise the ingenious treatment of the main rondo theme. Most of the remaining published cadenza sets can be divided conveniently into two main types: those which are largely compatible with the style and material of Beethoven's concerto, even if some of their harmonic, tonal and technical aspects belong to a different age; and those which, frankly, are not. David's substantial cadenzas for the first and last movements are stylistically appropriate yet provide ample opportunity for bravura display. Like Kreisler's, his eight-bar cadenza linking the slow movement and finale incorporates material from both movements. Léonard's cadenzas, as modified by Henri Marteau, are less effective, especially that for the first movement; but his cadenza for the Larghetto (seven bars) relates well to the material of the movement, while that for the finale (fourteen bars) is based firmly on the rondo theme.

Singer's and Auer's cadenzas for the first movement are founded appropriately on scales and arpeggios. Auer's, featuring primarily the timpani motive and the second theme, is one of the longest published cadenzas; like those of Laub, Schradieck, Heifetz and Jacobsen, it takes Joachim's as its model, while one extended chromatic scale passage of Singer's finds a precedent in Beethoven's first-movement cadenza for Op. 61a. Wilhelmj's extended cadenza to the first movement also finds inspiration in Beethoven's example for Op. 61a, alternating themes and figures from the movement with modulating sequences, but his pertinent cadenzas for the other two movements are brief and somewhat restrained. Flesch's cadenzas represent a serious attempt to develop Beethoven's musical ideas without emphasising virtuosity, but those for the outer movements are unstylishly chromatic and the second-movement cadenza combines material based on the Larghetto's closing statement with figuration which hints at the finale. Bezekirsky's cadenzas also suffer from awkward chromatic and harmonic treatment, and the frequent changes in rhythmic flow destroy the continuity of his cadenza for the finale, based chiefly on the horns' characteristic hunting fanfare at 3/46.

The more virtuosic cadenza sets by composer-violinists such as Vieuxtemps, Wieniawski, Hubay and Ysaÿe encompass virtually the entire range of the instrument and are often incompatible with the style and character of the concerto. Ysaÿe, who himself admitted, 'In original cadenzas by virtuosi, we find too much violin and too little music',[9] suffered the following criticism of his own anachronistic cadenzas: 'Those cadenzas of his, monstrous excrescences on the movements, nailed on, not grafted in, have no form, being merely examples of madly difficult ways of playing the themes that have been reasonably and beautifully presented by Beethoven. One's comfort is, that since Ysaÿe could hardly play them himself, nobody else is likely to be able to play them at all.'[10] Ysaÿe's twenty-four bar cadenza for the second movement adopts the 6/8 metre of the finale and uses figures which allude to it. Winkler's first-movement cadenza is incompatible in a very different way, for it is essentially an improvisation based on themes and gestures derived from Beethoven's string quartets!

Cadenzas by non-specialist violinists such as Saint-Saëns generally emphasise musical structure and tonal adventure rather than virtuoso display. Tovey makes a bold attempt to contrive musical links between the Larghetto and finale in his second-movement cadenza. Towards the end, an allusion to the main theme of the Larghetto is transformed gradually into a figure suggestive of the rondo theme; and his cadenza to the finale begins with a statement based on the horns' fanfare at 3/46 only to change to common time to introduce a Larghetto passage, with allusions to the second movement. Another tempo change to Allegro non troppo features arpeggios which allude in highly disguised fashion to the first movement's second theme. The Molto adagio conclusion cites the six notes prescribed by Beethoven for the end of the second-movement cadenza – quite a hotch-potch! Meanwhile, Busoni's first-movement cadenza, accompanied by strings and timpani from about its mid-point, is distinguished by a heavy reliance upon secondary material, with only one brief and somewhat disguised allusion to the movement's principal thematic substance. Curiously, his cadenza for the Larghetto avoids any allusion to its parent movement's material, incorporating instead the first movement's principal theme and ideas from the ensuing finale (notably at 3/68). His cadenza for the finale neglects the principal theme entirely, drawing instead on material from the second half of the second episode for two short variations, the second of which evolves into a brief development of the passagework at 3/81–91.

Cadenzas by contemporary musicians are often provocative but, predictably, suffer the wrath of most critics. Schnittke's first-movement cadenza, for example, has been criticised for its length (almost five minutes), 'its facile avant-garde effects – including what one supposes are imitations of electronic music – which are totally out of style',[11] and its incorporation of quotations from violin concertos by Brahms, Berg and Bartók. Furthermore, although Nigel Kennedy's cadenza for the finale (in his live recording with Tennstedt/N. German RSO) starts conventionally enough, its copious double stopping is essentially out of character with the concerto's violin idiom; and its later introduction of reminiscences of the principal themes of the first movement before lapsing into a curious atonal passage with quarter-tones establishes it as one of the most controversial of its kind. While these contemporary musicians and performers exhibit much originality, they have failed to create cadenzas whose content, style and character are consistent with those of the movement to which they relate. It has been left to the recent early music revival to encourage this welcome trend.

Appendix 1

Select discography
(in alphabetical order by artist)

The sheer number of meritorious recordings, past and present, of Beethoven's Violin Concerto causes problems in any assessment of overall and individual excellence. The recordings listed below represent, in the author's opinion, the twenty most outstanding performances in the work's recording history.

Violinist/orchestra/conductor	*Label & no.*
Accardo/Leipzig Gewandhaus/Masur	Philips 9500 407/7300 615
Busch, A./New York Philharmonic/ F. Busch	Brüder-Busch 12 PAL 3902/3
Chase/Hanover Band/Goodman	Cala Dig. CACD 1013
Ferras/Berlin Philharmonic/Karajan	DG SLPM 139021
Francescatti/Columbia Symphony/Walter	CBS SBRG 72006
Grumiaux/Concertgebouw/Davis	Philips 6500 775
Heifetz/Boston Symphony/Munch	HMV ALP1437
Hubermann/Vienna Philharmonic/Szell	Columbia LX 509/13
Krebbers/Concertgebouw/Haitink	Philips Sequenza 6527/7311
Kreisler/Berlin State Opera/Blech	HMV DB990–5 remastered: Biddulph LAB 049–50
Kulenkampff/Berlin Philharmonic/ Schmidt-Isserstedt	Telefunken E2016/21
Kyung-Wha Chung/Concertgebouw/ Tennstedt	EMI Dig. CDC7 54072–2
Menuhin/Philharmonia/Furtwängler	DB6574–9
Oistrakh, D./O National de la Radiodiffusion Française/Cluytens	HMV SXLP/TC-SXLP 30168
Perlman/Philharmonia/Giulini	HMV Dig. CDC 747002–2
Schneiderhan/Berlin Philharmonic/ van Kempen	DG LPM 18099
Stern/New York Philharmonic/Bernstein	CBS 60123/40

Szeryng/Concertgebouw/Haitink	Philips 6500 531
Szigeti/London Symphony/Dorati	Mercury MG 50358
Tetzlaff/SWF-Sinfonieorchester Baden Baden/Gielen	Sony CD 71008

Appendix 2

Published cadenzas for Beethoven's Violin Concerto

This appendix is intended both as a supplement to Chapter 7 and as a guide to the range of cadenzas available to the performer in printed format. Comprehensiveness is not its principal aim.

Abbado, Michelangelo	Milan, Ricordi, 1967
Auer, Leopold	Leipzig, Jul. Heinr. Zimmermann, 1901*
Bezekirsky, Vassily	Leipzig, P. Jürgenson, 1901
Bonavia, Ferruccio	London, Novello and Co., 1941
Busoni, Ferruccio	Leipzig, Breitkopf & Härtel, 1915/R Milan, Curci, 1963
David, Ferdinand	Leipzig, Breitkopf & Härtel, 1854
Dupuis, Jacques	Paris, S. Richault, c1860*
Flesch, Carl	New York, C. F. Peters, 1927
Gertler, André	Vienna, Universal, 1973
Giménez, Jerónimo	Madrid, Unión Musical Española, n.d.
Hellmesberger, Joseph Sen.	Vienna, Universal, 1901*
Herrmann, E.	Nuremberg, ?, 1883
Hilf, Arno	Leipzig, Forberg, 1909
Hubay, Jenö	Leipzig, Bosworth, 1895
Jacobsen, Maxim	Vienna, Universal, n.d.
Japha, Georg	Cologne, Tonger, 1888
Joachim, Joseph	2 sets: Vienna, Haslinger, 1853/R New York, International, 1945
Kreisler, Fritz	New York, Charles Foley, 1928
Laub, Ferdinand	Berlin, Heinrichshofen, 1859
Léonard, Hubert	Mainz, Schott, 1883
Meyer, Waldemar	Leipzig, Steingräber, 1902
Milstein, Nathan	New York, Schirmer, 1977
Novacek, Ottakar	Leipzig, Breitkopf & Härtel, 1899
Plotényi, Ferdinand	Mainz, Schott, 1887

Rostal, Max	London, Hawkes and Son, 1938
Saint-Saëns, Camille	Paris, Durand, 1898
Schneiderhan, Wolfgang	Munich, Henle, 1971
Schradieck, Henry	New York, Schirmer, 1895
Singer, Edmund	Leipzig, Kistner, 1857*
Spalding, Albert	Pittsburgh, Volkwein Brothers Inc., n.d.
Spivakovsky, Tossy	Wiesbaden, Breitkopf & Härtel, 1964
Spohr, Louis	London, Chanot, n.d.
Tovey, Donald	London, Oxford University Press, 1937
Vieuxtemps, Henri	Offenbach a. M., André, 1854
Wilhelmj, August	Berlin, Schlesinger, 1886
Winkler, Julius	Vienna, Doblinger, 1931
Ysaÿe, Eugène	rev. P. Newman: Brussels, Editions Ysaÿe, 1966

* first movement only

Appendix 3

Textual problems perpetuated in some printed scores

Note: this appendix is not intended as a substitute for the detailed observations on the sources normally included in a critical report.

1 Allegro ma non troppo

bb. 19, 21, 23, 119, 121, 401, 403: Only in b. 23 does Beethoven annotate dots over the final two quavers, and then only in the oboes. Many editors (e.g. Altmann) have extended dots to each of these bars, but Tyson adds dots to the other woodwind only in b. 23.

bb. 29, 31, 35 and parallel passages (bb. 225, 227, 231 and bb. 498, 500, 504): These passages are among the most controversial, making editors question whether Beethoven was simply careless in failing to bring the note-lengths into conformity or whether, at least at some stage in the gestation of the work, he intended to emphasise harmonic changes with a crotchet instead of a quaver at bb. 31, 227 and 500 and highlight the phrase ending/beginning at bb. 35, 231 and 504. The autograph suggests the latter, for bb. 29–35 are carefully annotated, with quavers in all relevant parts in b. 29, crotchets in b. 31, and crotchets in b. 35. The second passage (bb. 225–31) seems more hastily written with less care for detail, b. 225 giving quavers in every part and b. 227 likewise, except for the crotchet in the second violins, but b. 231 offering a mixture of ten quavers and three crotchets (hns, tpts and vcs/dbs); b. 498 also gives a real mixture of note-values (four quavers and six crotchets). Only the first violin part is written out in b. 500 (with the indication *come sopra* to cover the other instruments involved), so its quaver is of little significance in the argument, but b. 504 shows all parts in crotchets except the first violins. However, although it would appear that Beethoven intended these passages to be parallel (except in so far as certain instruments were precluded by the key of one of the passages from playing at all), the numerous inconsistencies of the first edition (Source C) regarding note-lengths in these bars have been perpetuated by several scores of our times.

bb. 35–8, 231–4, 504–7: In the autograph only the crotchets are marked *sf*, not the semiquavers or (in bb. 505/7) quavers. The *sf* marking is wrongly extended to all parts in Source B.

b. 63 (vc/db); bb. 166, 440 (vc): *arco*: This seems inconsistent but probably offers the most satisfactory solution. *Arco* in b. 63 is clear in the autograph and the temptation to make the other two passages agree with this first is confounded by the clarity of Beethoven's own pencil corrections in Source B (the autograph omits the *arco* indication in both places). That b. 63 is a tutti and bb. 166 and 440 are more delicate solo passages may provide a logical explanation for these inconsistencies.

b. 73: Inconsistencies in note-lengths on third beat (quaver or crotchet?), whereas bb. 74 and 268–9 give crotchets.

b. 75: The first flute note is an *a'''* not an *f♯'''* in the autograph; the *f♯'''*, reproduced in some modern scores, is an error derived from Source B.

b. 97 (vn solo): The hairpin derives from a pencil addition by Beethoven in Source B. A similar one was originally indicated at b. 292 but later crossed out.

bb. 128, 390: Clementi's inclusion in b. 128 of a grace note for the soloist, corresponding to those of bb. 126 and 130, provides one instance where his text is to be preferred to the autograph. Norman del Mar also points out that the equivalent grace note is present in the autograph at b. 388 but the one two bars later is missing. Although this seems capricious, he concludes that the omission of the appoggiatura over the same chord each time, though not in the identical place in the phrase, may mean that it is intentional and that the inclusion of both appoggiaturas in the normal violin copies is unjustified. The most sensible solution, however, is to include the ornament at each occurrence.

b. 191 and parallel passage at b. 465: Tyson ('The Textual Problems', p. 491) observes that a chord for oboe, clarinet and bassoons at b. 191, to correspond with that for oboes and clarinets at b. 465, was probably inadvertently omitted, as that bar formed the first of a new page of the autograph. He draws attention to the fact that the orchestration at b. 465 is, however, not beyond suspicion in the autograph, as the oboe parts were originally written on the flute's staff, and the clarinet parts in b. 465 were at some stage garbled in the autograph, probably after they had been copied for Clementi's edition. The traditional (first edition) text, in which the two passages are scored differently, is normally recommended.

b. 253: This bar and b. 257 underwent considerable alteration in the autograph. It would appear that notes 5–8 in b. 253 were originally *d' d' f' f'* with the equivalent in b. 257 *a a a a* ; b. 253 was later brought into conformity with b. 257; and then b. 257 was altered to *a a d' d'*, Beethoven presumably omitting to change b. 253 accordingly. The most satisfactory solution is to change b. 253 to comply with b. 257's *a a d' d'*.

bb. 274–83: Inadequate revisions, involving largely ambiguous deletions, in the autograph have raised doubts about the second bassoon's contribution in this passage. The most sensible and musical solution to the problem is for the second bassoon to slur bb. 278 and 279.

b. 301: The *espressivo* marking in the solo part of the autograph has been mis-interpreted in Source C as *sempre fortissimo*.

bb. 304–14: This passage has been subject to correction in the autograph, Beethoven's revisions (involving directives to instruments to follow another part) causing much confusion and further error: e.g. omission of second violins in bb. 305–6, failure to delete redundant cello part in b. 308, and cancellation of instructions to second violins (b. 314) and violas (bb. 312–14). Solution: second violins to double first violins in bb. 314–15; add violas (*col basso*) in bb. 312–14.

bb. 333–7: Szigeti perpetuates Beethoven's first version of the text by placing this passage an octave higher.

bb. 340, 342, 344: The solo violin part has no dots on the quavers in Sources A, B or D.

b. 341: There is confusion over whether the last three quavers of the solo part should be triplets. As triplets are not indicated as such ('3' markings are lacking throughout the piece), the length of the preceding rest provides the most infor-mative clue. Source B gives a crotchet rest, while Source C indicates a quaver rest. The autograph includes two versions, both preceded by a crotchet rest, thus turning the tide of preference for triplet quavers.

bb. 365–85, 497–509: The Peters and Philharmonia scores indicate that the soloist should play along with the tutti in just these two passages. Source B shows clearly how this originated, but the autograph is absolutely clear in giving rests.

b. 369: The flute note should be a crotchet (as in the autograph), not a quaver (as in Source B).

bb. 482–3 (vn solo): No tie in the autograph or Source B; clearly a new trill is required.

bb. 495–6: The viola part originally comprised two tied *a'*s in these bars. When b. 496 was altered to *e'*, the tie, which probably should no longer apply, was never deleted. Source B gives it (as slur) but misprints b. 495 as *c#'*!

A3.1 Beethoven: Violin Concerto in D major Op. 61 (1st movement), showing the important cello line omitted from some scores

bb. 523–4: Tyson admits that the cellos should really play *col basso* here (as Sources A and B clearly confirm), but omits to incorporate it in his text, doubtless because the resultant part writing offends.

bb. 525–35: Some critical editions (e.g. that of Wilhelm Altmann for Eulenburg, and the Boosey & Hawkes and Philharmonia ('Revision 1960') miniature scores) omit the cello line given in the autograph (Ex. A3.1), following instead the first edition (Source C) and requiring the cellos to 'double' the simple bass line instead. Reference to Source B verifies that the cello part of the autograph should stand and reveals how it came to be omitted from the first edition engraved from it.

b. 526: The controversy here is whether the last note of the solo part should be a *c♯″* (as in Source B) or an *e″* (as in Source C). The autograph's variants also beg to differ, the triplet version adopted by the violin including an *e″* and the semiquaver version adopted by the piano giving a *c♯″*. An *e″* seems the more logical solution.

2 Larghetto

bb. 21–7: The pizzicato note-lengths are inconsistent in the autograph. The most sensible solution is to use quavers throughout.

b. 40: Some modern editions incorrectly give the soloist a quaver *g′* (with the first violins) at the beginning of the bar.

3 Rondo: Allegro

bb. 1–26: Many performances make a special feature of the fact that, in printed scores, the *g′* in b. 2 of the solo part has no dot whereas the final notes of bb. 0

and 1 include dots. The *g'* is then played long and the resultant variety in style can be effective. However, there is little evidence for this in the sources. Beethoven tends not to write a dot on this *g'* (he does once in b. 16), but the other final notes rarely have dots either. The only dot he is fairly consistent about is, as modern scores show in bb. 256–66, on the second note of the bar, whether slurred (bb. 1, 2; N.B.!) or not (bb. 11,12). However, there is a clear dot in the solo violin part in b. 10, and probably also on the first note of the piece and this could be taken as warranting similar dots on the final notes of bb. 1 and 2 etc. Furthermore, Source B is differently inconsistent, so the most logical solution is to retain the dots Beethoven seemed to write in the autograph with some consistency.

b. 9 (hns): The third note is actually a crotchet, not a quaver.

b. 24: The length of the fourth note is inconsistent.

bb. 41–3 and parallel passage at bb. 214–16: The original omission of the viola part in the autograph (bb. 41–3) has been remedied in Sources B (by Beethoven in pencil) and C by requiring the violas to double the cellos, as in the previous four bars. Beethoven's subsequent addition of a viola part to the autograph is similar but at the lower octave.

b. 54 (bns): The upbeat to b. 55 should probably be restored.

bb. 60 and 64, 235 and 239: The length of the last notes in the orchestral parts is inconsistent in the autograph, followed identically by Source B; bb. 60 and 235 are consistently quavers and it is normal practice to bring b. 64 (all crotchets in the autograph) and b. 239 (a mixture of crotchets and quavers in the autograph) into line with this. The slurs/ties are even more chaotic here.

bb. 68–73 and parallel passage bb. 243–8 (hns): Reference to the autograph reveals inconsistencies in the ties and the omission of a note in b. 73, at the beginning of a new page (Ex. A3.2). This omission was restored inaccurately by Beethoven at proof stage – he added crotchets instead of quavers. The most practical solution is to add quavers in the horn parts in b. 73 and mirror the ties of bb. 68–73 in bb. 243–8.

b. 72 (vas): The rest is confirmed, but this silent bar may be an oversight.

b. 83: The soloist should probably play an octave higher than in the traditional version that has come down to us, thereby bringing bb. 83–4 into concordance with bb. 81–2 (and, indeed, the right hand of the piano transcription).

bb. 86–91: This passage has undergone much revision in the autograph, especially in the first violins, flute and bassoons. Originally the flute probably

A3.2 Beethoven: Violin Concerto in D major Op. 61 (3rd movement), showing the inconsistencies in the ties of the horn part and the omission of notes in bar 73 of the autograph

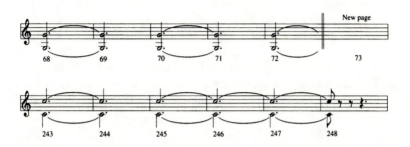

doubled the first violins at the octave; in any case the flute played g''s in 86–91, those in bb. 87, 88 and 89 being tied. Beethoven's revisions in the autograph involved the deletion of the g''s in bb. 86, 87, 89, 90 and 91, but he left the g'' in b. 88, together with the ties from b. 87 and to b. 89. The copyist for Source B retained the g'' at b. 88, including also the nonsensical tie to b. 89 (a bar's rest!), and this misunderstanding has been perpetuated in most subsequent editions. Interestingly, the copyist of the set of parts on which Source C is based deleted the g'' at 88, probably correctly.

b. 152 (vn solo): In all sources note 8 is an $a\natural'$ but must be an ab'.

bb. 216–18: Some critical editions (e.g. that of Wilhelm Altmann for Eulenburg) follow Sources B and C and omit a bar at b. 217, whereas the accepted solution is to bring the passage in line with its parallel material in bb. 43–5. Tyson ('The Text', p. 112) provides a full explanation for the error, which derives from mistaken interpretation of Beethoven's 'shorthand' in the autograph. The pizzicato variant for the soloist (b. 218) seems to have been an afterthought of the composer.

b. 233 (cl): Clearly a written c'' not an e'' as in Sources A and B.

b. 265: All sources have f on the final quaver, but this should have been deleted.

b. 335 (2nd hn): The first note is a written c' in all sources despite the contents of b. 329.

Finally, Tyson ('The Textual Problems', pp. 497–8) notes that Beethoven's frequent bowing/phrasing slurs and staccato marks are open to a variety of interpretations; he also highlights a number of instances of indiscriminate dynamic additions in the orchestral parts of Source B, which were doubtless unauthorised by the composer and have filtered through into many published editions. These include:

1/50   Beethoven's careful distinction between the dynamic markings for trumpets (*pp*), horns (*p*) and timpani (*sempre p*) in the autograph is counteracted by a blanket *pp* in all three orchestral sections in Source B.

2/11, 20 the clarinet (b. 11) and bassoon (b. 20) only are marked *dolce* in the autograph, whereas this term is added to the accompanying parts as well in Source B.

Notes

1 Towards the Violin Concerto Op. 61

1. Letter of 29 June 1801, in Anderson (ed.), *The Letters*, no. 51, I, p. 58.
2. Solomon, *Beethoven Essays*, pp. 116–25.
3. See, for example, W. W. Cobbett, *Cyclopedic Survey of Chamber Music* (2 vols., Oxford, 1929), I, art. 'Beethoven'.
4. in Sonneck, *Beethoven*, p. 31.
5. Tyson, 'Beethoven's Heroic Phase', pp. 139–41.
6. Broyles, *The Emergence*, p. 98.
7. See also Junker on Beethoven's improvisation in Forbes (ed.), *Thayer's Life*, p. 105.
8. *Ibid.*, pp. 57–8.
9. Ries and Wegeler, *Biographische Notizen*, p. 141; Solomon, *Beethoven*, p. 99.
10. Ries and Wegeler, *Biographische Notizen*, p. 141.
11. Breuning, *Memories*, ed. Solomon, pp. 28–9.
12. H. B. Cox and C. L. E. Cox (eds.), *Leaves from the Journals of Sir George Smart* (London, 1907), p. 109.
13. 'scritta in un stilo molto concertante, quasi come d'un concerto'; see Schwarz, 'Beethoven and the French Violin School', p. 440, n. 32.
14. A facsimile may be found in Schiedermair, *Der junge Beethoven*, pp. 427–78; a piano reduction setting from the old Hellmesberger version appears in *The Violexchange* 1/4 (1986), pp. 26–31.
15. in Arnold and Fortune (eds.), *The Beethoven Companion*, pp. 318–19.
16. Fischer, Preface to his edition (Bärenreiter, 1972), trans. M. Bent; see supplements to the *Beethoven-Gesamtausgabe* III/1 (Wiesbaden, 1961) and also Kinsky, *Das Werk Beethovens*, ed. Halm, p. 434.
17. Cooper (ed.), *The Beethoven Compendium*, p. 220.
18. in Arnold and Fortune (eds.), *The Beethoven Companion*, p. 318.
19. as *Konzertstück für Violine und Orchester* (Universal Edition, 1943?).

20. Manén's orchestration is for flute, two oboes, two bassoons, two horns and strings, with violas non divisi.
21. Tovey, *Beethoven*, p. 105.
22. Fischer has therefore supplied only bars 260–1; 266–81; 376–8; and 399–401. These figures do not take into account the overlong, unstylish cadenza by Takaya Urakawa included in this edition.
23. See R. Stowell, *Violin Technique and Performance Practice in the Late Eighteenth and Early Nineteenth Centuries* (Cambridge, 1985), pp. 23–31; D. D. Boyden, *The History of Violin Playing from its Origins to 1761* (London, 1965/R1975), pp. 317–24; D. Gill (ed.), *The Book of the Violin* (Oxford, 1984), pp. 17–47.
24. See W. H., A. F. and A. E. Hill, *Antonio Stradivari: His Life and Work* (London, 1902; 2nd edn, 1909/R1963), p. 188.
25. See L. Spohr, *Violinschule* (Vienna, 1832), p. 13; P. Baillot, *L'art du Violon* (Paris, 1835), p. 16.
26. See Segerman, 'Strings'; Abbot and Segerman, 'Gut Strings'; Gill (ed.), *The Book of the Violin*, pp. 37–43; and S. Bonta, 'Catline Strings Revisited', *Journal of the American Musical Instrument Society* 14 (1988), pp. 38–60.
27. F.-J. Gossec, *Procès-verbaux de l'Académie des beaux-arts*, ed. M. Bonnaire (Paris, 1937), I, pp. 156–61; in A. Cohen, 'A Cache of 18th-century Strings', *Galpin Society Journal* 36 (1983), pp. 38–9.
28. See Stowell, *Violin Technique*, pp. 11–23; Boyden, *The History of Violin Playing*, pp. 324–30; Boyden, 'The Violin Bow'; R. Stowell, 'Violin Bowing in Transition', *Early Music* 12 (1984), pp. 317–27.
29. J. Roda, *Bows for Musical Instruments of the Violin Family* (Chicago, 1959), p. 65.
30. Letter of 4 October 1804, in Anderson (ed.), *The Letters*, no. 99, I, pp. 119–20.
31. See Solomon, *Beethoven*, pp. 130–1.
32. in Jander, 'The "Kreutzer" Sonata', p. 37.
33. L. Mozart, *Versuch einer gründlichen Violinschule* (Augsburg 1756/R1976), p. 102.
34. M. Woldemar, *Méthode de violon par L. Mozart rédigée par Woldemar...*(Paris, 1801), p. 5.
35. R. Winter and R. Martin (eds.), *The Beethoven Quartet Companion* (California, 1994), pp. 32–3.
36. *Allgemeine Musikalische Zeitung* 7 (1805), col. 500.

2 The genesis of Op. 61

1. A. Schmitz, for example, in his *Beethoven* (Bonn, 1927) established many parallels between Beethoven's music and the works of Gossec, Grétry, Kreutzer, Berton, Méhul, Catel and Cherubini. See also Schwarz, *French Instrumental Music*.

2. F. J. Fétis (ed.), *Biographie Universelle des musiciens et bibliographie générale de la musique* (8 vols., Brussels, 1835–44, 2nd edition, 1860–5/R1963), VII, p. 246.

3. P. Baillot, *Notice sur Viotti* (Paris, 1825).

4. Schering, *Geschichte*, p. 204.

5. Schwarz, 'Beethoven and the French Violin School', p. 432.

6. Letter of 4 October 1804, in Anderson (ed.), *The Letters*, no. 99, I, pp. 119–20.

7. H. Berlioz, *Voyage musical en Allemagne et en Italie* (Paris, 1844), p. 263.

8. Spohr, *Autobiography*, Eng. trans. (2nd edn, 2 vols., London, 1878), I, p. 165.

9. Letter of 29? December 1812, in Anderson (ed.), *The Letters*, no. 392, I, pp. 391–2.

10. *Gloggl's Musikzeitung*, 4 January 1813; in Schwarz, 'Beethoven and the French Violin School', p. 441.

11. See Broyles, *The Emergence*, pp. 123–4.

12. A. Einstein, 'The Military Element in Beethoven', *Monthly Musical Record* 61 (1939), p. 271.

13. Schering, *Geschichte*, p. 169.

14. A. Einstein, *Mozart* (New York, 1945), p. 282.

15. Schwarz, 'Beethoven and the French Violin School', pp. 436–7.

16. *Ibid.*, pp. 443–7.

17. J. La Rue, E. Wellesz and F. W. Sternfeld, in *The New Oxford History of Music* (14 vols., London, 1954–), VII, p. 487.

18. Beda Plank diary entry (25 March 1801) in H. C. Robbins Landon, *Haydn: Chronicle and Works* (5 vols., London, 1976–80), V, p. 31.

19. A. Ysaÿe, *Eugène Ysaÿe* (Brussels, 1974), pp. 393–4.

20. *Wiener Zeitung*, 1793, pp. 559, 791; and 1794, pp. 704, 828; in Haas, 'The Viennese Violinist', p. 21.

21. Haas, 'The Viennese Violinist', pp. 23–4.

22. in G. Schilling, *Encyklopädie der gesammten musikalischen Wissenschaften oder Universal Lexikon der Tonkunst* (6 vols., Stuttgart, 1835–8/R1973), II, art. 'Clement'.

23. *Allgemeine Musikalische Zeitung* 7 (1805), col. 500.

24. *Allgemeine Musikalische Zeitung* 15 (1813), col. 400; and 35 (1833), col. 397.

25 cited in Haas, 'The Viennese Violinist', p. 22.
26. Forbes (ed.), *Thayer's Life*, pp. 122–4.
27. C. Czerny, *Vollständige theoretisch-praktische Pianoforte-Schule* Op. 500 (4 vols., Vienna, 1846), IV, p. 117.
28. Spohr, *Autobiography*, I, p. 175.
29. Haas, 'The Viennese Violinist', p. 23.
30. Schering, *Geschichte*, p. 204.
31. I must acknowledge here a considerable debt to Clive Brown, whose BBC Radio 3 'Music Weekly' broadcast on 7 May 1989 inspired me to further investigation.
32. *Allgemeine Musikalische Zeitung* 7 (1805), col. 500.

3 Reception and performance history

1. See M. S. Morrow, *Concert Life in Haydn's Vienna* (New York, 1989); O. Biba, 'Concert Life in Beethoven's Vienna', in R. Winter and B. Carr (eds.), *Beethoven, Performers, and Critics* (Detroit, 1980), pp. 77–93.
2. *Wiener Zeitung für Theater Musik und Poesie* 2 (1807), col. 27.
3. R. Wallace, *Beethoven's Critics: Aesthetic Dilemmas and Resolutions during the Composer's Lifetime* (Cambridge, 1986), p. 5.
4. *Allgemeine Musikalische Zeitung* 9 (1807), col. 235.
5. Wallace, *Beethoven's Critics*, p. 7.
6. A. Schindler, *Biographie von Ludwig van Beethoven* (Münster, 1871/R1970), p. 140.
7. *Allgemeine Musikalische Zeitung* 26 (1824), col. 366; and 35 (1833), col. 397.
8. *Allgemeine Musikalische Zeitung* 31 (1829), col. 379.
9. in Moser, *Joseph Joachim*, II, p. 290.
10. *The Morning Post*, 28 May 1844; in Moser, *Joseph Joachim*, II, p. 60.
11. my italics; Preface to Jacob Dont's edition of Beethoven's Violin Concerto (Berlin, Schlesinger, c1880), cited in C. Brown, 'Ferdinand David's Editions of Beethoven', in Stowell (ed.), *Performing Beethoven*, pp. 124–5.
12. Pincherle, 'Le Concerto', p. 82.
13. *Revue Musicale* 3 (1828), p. 205.
14. See *Allgemeine Musikalische Zeitung* 49 (1847), col. 118.
15. *Allgemeine Musikalische Zeitung* 35 (1833), col. 113; and 43 (1841), cols. 195–6.
16. See *Allgemeine Musikalische Zeitung* 43 (1841), col. 228; 44 (1842), col. 941; 46 (1844), col. 428.
17. *The Athenaeum*, 14 April 1832, p. 245; *The Harmonicon*, May 1832, p. 117.

18. A. Ysaÿe & B. Ratcliffe, *Ysaÿe, His Life, Work and Influence* (London, 1947), pp. 211–12.

19. See Moser, *Joseph Joachim*, p. 56.

20. *The Musical World* 19/22 (1844), pp. 179–81; *The Morning Post*, 28 May 1844, in Moser, *Joseph Joachim*, p. 60; in Fuller-Maitland, *Joachim*, pp. 9–11.

21. B. Litzmann, *Clara Schumann: ein Künstlerleben* (3 vols., Leipzig, 1902–8) II, pp. 111–12.

22. Moser, *Joseph Joachim*, p. 31; Schwarz, *Great Masters*, p. 214.

23. *Allgemeine Musikalische Zeitung* 36 (1834), col. 418; Schwarz, *Great Masters*, p. 211.

24. *Allgemeine Musikalische Zeitung* 45 (1843), col. 603; Hanslick, *Vienna's Golden Years*, p. 37.

25. Hanslick, *Vienna's Golden Years*, p. 77.

26. M. Smith, *The Life of Ole Bull* (New York, 1943), p. 194.

27. See Revd. J. E. Cox, *Musical Recollections of the Last Half-Century* (2 vols., London, 1872), I, pp. 196–7.

28. See *Revue et Gazette Musicale*, 5 November 1876 and 5 March 1876.

29. Flesch, *Memoirs*, p. 39; in L. Ginsburg, *Ysaÿe*, trans. X. M. Dando and ed. H. Axelrod (Neptune City, N.J., 1980), p. 379.

30. Flesch, *Memoirs*, p. 84.

31. in S. Sadie (ed.), *New Grove Dictionary* (20 vols., London, 1980), VI, art. 'Flesch, Carl'; see Flesch, *Memoirs*, p. 247n.

32. Sadie (ed.), *New Grove Dictionary*, XX, art. 'Ysaÿe, Eugène'.

33. Schwarz, *Great Masters*, p. 291; A. Ysaÿe, *Eugène Ysaÿe* (Brussels, 1974), pp. 393–4.

34. Flesch, *Memoirs*, p. 80; *The World*, 6 May 1891.

35. Kaskin after Ysaÿe's performance of the Beethoven Concerto on 12 December 1905; in Ginsburg, *Ysaÿe*, p. 397.

36. See R. Philip, *Early Recordings*. A select discography of recordings of the concerto is given as Appendix 1.

37. Sadie (ed.), *New Grove Dictionary*, X, art. 'Kulenkampff, Georg'.

38. Flesch, *Memoirs*, p. 292.

39. Sadie (ed.), *New Grove Dictionary*, X, art. 'Kogan, Leonid'.

40. Schwarz, *Great Masters*, p. 403.

41. I. March (ed.), *The Complete Penguin Stereo Record and Cassette Guide* (Harmondsworth, 1984), p. 97.

42. See R. Stowell, 'The Violin Concerto Op. 61', in Stowell (ed.), *Performing Beethoven*, pp. 150–94.

43. A. Bachmann, *An Encyclopedia of the Violin* (New York, 1925/R1966), p. 224.
44. For example, Flesch, *The Art of Violin Playing*; I. Galamian, *Principles of Violin Playing and Teaching* (Englewood Cliffs, N.J., 1962); J. Szigeti, *Szigeti on the Violin* (London, 1969).
45. (Wiesbaden, Breitkopf & Härtel, [1969]). Hess includes the variants as well as a few editorial slurs in his edition.
46. Max Rostal, Preface to his edition (Mainz, B. Schott's Söhne, 1971).
47. See Brown, 'Ferdinand David's Editions', pp. 117–49.
48. *Ibid.*, p. 122–3.
49. See Stowell, 'The Violin Concerto Op. 61', pp. 156–7.
50. Bachmann, *Encyclopedia of the Violin*, p. 225.
51. Moser, *Geschichte des Violinspiels*, II, p. 148.
52. Brown, 'Ferdinand David's Editions', p. 126.
53. Ries and Wegeler, *Biographische Notizen*, pp. 120–1.
54. Tyson, *The Authentic English Editions*, pp. 51–2.
55. See White, 'Did Viotti Write?'
56. Cooper (ed.), *The Beethoven Compendium*, p. 272.
57. in Tyson, 'The Text', p. 105.
58. See Forbes (ed.), *Thayer's Life*, p. 302.
59. Kaiser, 'Die authentischen Fassungen'.
60. Letter of 6 February 1816, in Anderson (ed.), *The Letters*, no. 606a, II, p. 557.
61. in A. Tyson, 'Music Reviews: Beethoven's Op. 61', *Musical Times* 111 (1970), p. 827.
62. Anderson (ed.), *The Letters*, nos.142–6 and 150, I, pp. 167–72 and 174.
63. Del Mar, *Conducting Beethoven*, II, p. 107.

4 The textual history

1. Concerto written by clemency for Clement [lit.], First violin and Director of the Vienna Court Theatre, by Ludwig van Beethoven, 1806; Tovey, *Essays*, III, p. 87.
2. See Kinsky, 'Zur Versteigerung', p. 66. A. Tyson's 'Sketches and Autographs', in Arnold and Fortune (eds.), *The Beethoven Companion*, pp. 443–58 is recommended as a useful introduction to the types and different functions of Beethoven's sketchbooks.
3. Cooper, *Beethoven and the Creative Process*, p. 80; p. 116.
4. For further discussion of these sources see Mies, 'Die Quellen', p. 193; Tyson, 'The Text', pp. 104–14; Tyson, 'The Textual Problems', pp. 482–502; Kaiser, 'Die authentischen Fassungen', pp. 196–8.

5. Reference has been made to the *Vollständige Faksimile-Ausgabe im Original-format der Handschrift aus dem Besitz der Österreichischen Nationalbibliothek* (Mus. Hs. 17.538). Herausgegeben und kommentiert von Franz Grasberger. Mit einem Vorwort von Wolfgang Schneiderhan (2 vols., Graz, Akademische Druck- u. Verlagsanstalt, 1979).

6. Tyson, 'The Textual Problems', p. 483.

7. C. Czerny, *Vollständige theoretisch-praktische Pianoforte-Schule* Op. 500 (Vienna, 1846), IV, p. 117.

8. See Tyson, 'The Textual Problems', pp. 484–5.

9. For details see Kinsky, *Das Werk Beethovens*, pp. 147–9.

10. See Tyson, *The Authentic English Editions*, pp. 55–8.

11. Tyson, 'The Textual Problems', p. 487. In 'The Text', pp. 113–14, Tyson substantiates this claim that Clementi's edition (Source D) is related to the autograph (or a copy taken from it) and as such 'precedes' the first edition, citing relevant examples, largely involving dynamic indications, from the slow movement.

12. Jahn, 'Beethoven und die Ausgaben', p. 325; Nottebohm, *Zweite Beethoveniana*, p. 587; Jonas, 'Das Autograph', pp. 443f.

13. Kaiser, 'Die authentischen Fassungen', pp. 196ff.; W. Hess, *Beethoven, Supplemente zur Gesamtausgabe X: Werke für Soloinstrumente und Orchester*, vol. II (Wiesbaden, 1969).

14. Kojima, 'Die Solovioline-Fassungen', pp. 101ff.

15. See Anderson, *The Letters*, nos. 134 and 137, I, pp. 152–3 and 156–7.

16. *Ibid.*, no. 141, I, pp. 166–7. This letter was written in another hand but signed by Beethoven.

17. *Ibid.*, no. 142, I, p. 167.

18. In A. W. Thayer, *Ludwig van Beethovens Leben* (3 vols., Berlin, 1866–79; vol. I rev. H. Deiters, Berlin, 1901, rev. H. Riemann, 1917; vols. II–III rev. H. Riemann, Leipzig, 1910–11; vols. IV–V, continued and completed by H. Deiters and H. Riemann, rev. Riemann, Leipzig 1907–8; vols. II–V reissued, Leipzig. 1922–3), II, 538.

19. W. Drabkin, 'Begging to Differ', *Musical Times* 135 (1994), p. 759.

20. Tyson, 'The Text', p. 112.

21. Del Mar, 'Confusion and Error'; Del Mar, *Conducting Beethoven*, II, pp. 100–14; Tyson, 'The Text'; Tyson, 'The Textual Problems'.

5 Structure and style I – 1. Allegro ma non troppo

1. R. Magidoff, *Yehudi Menuhin* (New York, 1955), p. 69.

2. C. Rosen, *The Classical Style* (New York, 1971), pp. 257–8.

3. Tovey, *Essays*, III, p. 88.
4. in J. Joachim and A. Moser, *Violinschule* (2 vols., Berlin, 1902–5), trans. A. Moffat (3 vols., Berlin and Leipzig, 1907), III, p. 181.
5. Tovey, *Essays*, III, p. 89.
6. in R. Layton (ed.), *A Companion to the Concerto* (London, 1988), p. 122.
7. P. Williams, *The Chromatic Fourth during Four Centuries of Music* (Oxford, forthcoming).
8. Tovey, *Beethoven*, pp. 116–17.
9. Fiske, *Beethoven Concertos*, p. 31.
10. Spohr, *Violinschule* (Vienna, 1832), p. 196.

6 Structure and style II – 2/3. Larghetto – Rondo: Allegro

1. Wallace, *Beethoven's Critics*, p. 14.
2. Y. Menuhin and W. Primrose, *Violin and Viola* (London, 1976), pp. 123–4.
3. Del Mar, *Conducting Beethoven*, II, p. 110. Del Mar points out that this melodic line resembles closely 1/18–19 and equivalent places in the movement.
4. designated Andante in Op. 61a. Czerny suggests a metronome marking of $\downarrow = 60$.
5. Tovey, *Essays*, III, p. 93; Fiske, *Beethoven Concertos*, p. 31; Moser, 'Die Form'.
6. Grove, 'Beethoven's Violin Concerto', p. 469; Arnold and Fortune (eds.), *The Beethoven Companion*, p. 325; Cooper (ed.), *The Beethoven Compendium*, p. 219.
7. A. Hopkins, *Talking About Concertos* (London, 1964), p. 56.
8. Interestingly, the first and second violin parts at 2/87–8 of Clementi's edition are marked 'uno Violino', corresponding to a similar indication in the autograph subsequently crossed out. Tyson (*The Authentic English Editions*, pp. 56–7) lists other unique features of Clementi's editions.
9. Jander, 'Romantic Form and Content'. I must here acknowledge my debt to Jander's article for much of this material concerning the slow movement.
10. H. C. Koch, *Versuch einer Anleitung zur Composition* (4 vols., Rudolstadt and Leipzig, 1782–93/R1969), III, p. 340, and IV, p. 111.
11. See S. Sadie (ed.), *New Grove Dictionary* (20 vols., London, 1980), XVI, art. 'Romance'.
12. Jander, 'Romantic Form and Content', p. 162; J. J. Rousseau, *Dictionnaire de Musique* (Paris, 1768), art. 'Romance'.
13. Jander, 'Romantic Form and Content', pp. 164–9.
14. *Ibid.*, p. 171.

15. See, for example, Jander, 'The "Kreutzer" Sonata'.
16. Jander, 'Romantic Form and Content', p. 178.
17. Czerny suggests a metronome marking of ♩ = 100.
18. Kinderman, *Beethoven*, p. 24.
19. Schering, *Geschichte*, p. 204.

7 Cadenzas

1. See Swain, 'Form and Function', p. 37.
2. See Cooper, *Beethoven and the Creative Process*, p. 303.
3. *Allgemeine Musikalische Zeitung* 7 (1805), cols. 242–3.
4. D. Tovey, 'Prefaces to Cadenzas for Classical Concertos', in D. Tovey, *Essays and Lectures* (London, 1949), p. 321.
5. Whitmore, *Unpremeditated Art*, p. 199.
6. See Appendix 2. In addition, several cadenzas have been 'published' in recorded, as opposed to printed, format. Ruggiero Ricci's recent recording of the concerto includes performances of fourteen different cadenzas.
7. L. P. Lochner, *Fritz Kreisler* (London, 1951), p. 38.
8. Del Mar, *Conducting Beethoven*, II, p. 111; and Menuhin quoted in Fiske, *Beethoven Concertos*, p. 32.
9. L. Ginsburg, *Ysaÿe*, trans. X. M. Dando and ed. H. Axelrod (Neptune City, N.J., 1980), p. 539.
10. *The World*, 6 May 1891.
11. I. March (ed.), *The Complete Penguin Stereo Record and Cassette Guide* (Harmondsworth, 1984), p. 99.

Select bibliography

Abbot, D., and Segerman, E., 'Gut Strings', *Early Music* 4 (1976), pp. 430–7

Anderson, E. (ed.), *The Letters of Beethoven* (3 vols., London, 1961)

Arnold, D., and Fortune, N. (eds.), *The Beethoven Companion* (London, 1971)

Boyden, D. D., 'The Violin Bow in the Eighteenth Century', *Early Music* 8 (1980), pp. 199–212

Breuning, G. von, *Memories of Beethoven*, ed. M. Solomon (Cambridge, 1992)

Broyles, M., *The Emergence and Evolution of Beethoven's Heroic Style* (New York, 1987)

Cooper, B., *Beethoven and the Creative Process* (Oxford, 1990)

Cooper, B. (ed.), *The Beethoven Compendium. A Guide to Beethoven's Life and Music* (London, 1991)

Creighton, J., *The Discopaedia of the Violin 1889–1971* (Toronto and Buffalo, 1974)

Del Mar, N., 'Confusion and Error (III)', *The Score* 20 (1958), pp. 38–40
Conducting Beethoven, vol. II: *Overtures, Concertos, Missa Solemnis* (Oxford, 1993)

Emery, F. B., *The Violin Concerto* (Chicago, 1920)

Fiske, R., *Beethoven Concertos and Overtures* (London, 1970)

Flesch, C., *The Memoirs of Carl Flesch*, trans. and ed. H. Keller (London, 1957)
Die Kunst des Violin-Spiels (2 vols., Berlin, 1923–8); trans. F. H. Martens as *The Art of Violin Playing*, (2 vols., New York, 1924–30)

Forbes, E. (ed.), *Thayer's Life of Beethoven* (2nd edn, Princeton, 1967)

Fuller-Maitland, J., *Joachim* (London and New York, 1905)

Grove, G., 'Beethoven's Violin Concerto (Op. 61.)', *Musical Times* 46 (1905), pp. 459–71

Haas, R., 'The Viennese Violinist, Franz Clement', *Musical Quarterly* 34 (1948), pp. 15–27

Hanslick, E., *Vienna's Golden Years of Music 1850–1900*, trans. and ed. H. Pleasants (New York, 1950)

Hess, W., 'Die verschiedenen Fassungen von Beethovens Violinkonzert', *Schweizerische Musikzeitung* 109 (1969), pp. 197–201

'Die Originalkadenzen zu Beethovens Klavierkonzerten', *Schweizerische Musikzeitung* 112 (1972), pp. 270–5

Jahn, O., 'Beethoven und die Ausgaben seiner Werke', in *Gesammelte Aufsätze über Musik* (Leipzig, 1867), pp. 271–333

Jander, O., 'The "Kreutzer" Sonata as Dialogue', *Early Music* 16 (1988), pp. 34–49

'Romantic Form and Content in the Slow Movement of Beethoven's Violin Concerto', *Musical Quarterly* 69 (1983), pp. 159–79

Jonas, O., 'Das Autograph von Beethovens Violinkonzert', *Zeitschrift für Musikwissenschaft* 13 (1930/31), pp. 443–50

Kaiser, F., 'Die authentischen Fassungen des D-dur-Konzertes Op. 61 von Ludwig van Beethoven', in *Bericht über den internationalen musikwissenschaftlichen Kongress Kassel 1962* (Kassel, 1963), pp. 196–8

Kinderman, W., *Beethoven* (Oxford, 1995)

Kinsky, G., *Das Werk Beethovens*, ed. H. Halm (Munich, 1955)

'Zur Versteigerung von Beethovens musikalischem Nachlass', *Neues Beethoven-Jahrbuch* 6 (1935), pp. 66–86

Kojima, S.A., 'Die Solovioline-Fassungen und -Varianten von Beethovens Violinkonzert Op. 61 – ihre Entstehung und Bedeutung', *Beethoven Jahrbuch* 8 (1971–2), pp. 97–145

Kolisch, R., and Leibowitz, R., 'Aufführungsprobleme im Violinkonzert von Beethoven', *Musica* 33 (1979), pp. 148–55

Kross, S., 'Improvisation und Konzertform bei Beethoven', *Beethoven-Kolloquium 1977*, ed. R. Klein (Kassel, 1978), pp. 132–9

Laurencie, L. de la, *L'école française de violon de Lully à Viotti* (3 vols., Paris, 1922–4/R Geneva, 1971)

Lenz, W. von, *Beethoven et ses trois styles: analyses des sonates de piano suivies de l'essai d'un catalogue critique chronologique et anecdotique de l'œuvre de Beethoven* (St Petersburg, 1852); ed. M. D. Calvocoressi (Paris, 1906)

Lockwood, L., 'On Beethoven's Sketches and Autographs: Some Problems of Definition and Interpretation', *Acta Musicologica* 42 (1970), pp. 32–47

Lockwood L., and Benjamin, P. (eds.), *Beethoven Essays: Studies in Honor of Elliot Forbes* (Cambridge, Mass., 1984)

Mies, P., 'Die Quellen des Op. 61 von Ludwig van Beethoven', in *Bericht über den siebenten internationalen musikwissenschaftlichen Kongress Köln 1958* (Kassel, 1959), pp. 193–5

Mohr, W., 'Die Klavierfassung von Beethovens Violinkonzert', *Österreichische Musikzeitschrift* 27 (1972), pp. 71–5

Moser, A., *Joseph Joachim, ein Lebensbild* (Berlin, 1910)

Geschichte des Violinspiels (2 vols., Berlin, 1923; 2nd rev. edn, Tutzing, 1966–7)

Moser, H. J., 'Die Form des Beethovenschen Violinkonzerts', *Neues Beethoven-Jahrbuch* 9 (1939), pp. 16–25

Munter, F., 'Beethovens Bearbeitungen eigener Werke', *Neues Beethoven-Jahrbuch* 6 (1935), pp. 159–73

Neurath, H., 'Das Violinkonzert in der Wiener klassischen Schule', *Studien zur Musikwissenschaft* 14 (1927) pp. 125–42

Nottebohm, G., *Zweite Beethoveniana* (Leipzig, 1887)

Philip, R., *Early Recordings and Musical Style: Changing Tastes in Instrumental Performance, 1900–1950* (Cambridge, 1992)

Pincherle, M., 'Le Concerto de Violon de Beethoven', *La Revue Musicale* 8 (1927), pp. 77–83

Reynolds, C., Lockwood, L., and Webster, J. (eds.), *Beethoven Forum 1* (Lincoln, Nebr. and London, 1992)

Ries, F., and Wegeler, F., *Biographische Notizen über Ludwig van Beethoven*, ed. A. C. Kalischer (Berlin, 1906)

Sadie, S. (ed.), *New Grove Dictionary of Music and Musicians* (20 vols., London, 1980)

Schering, A., *Die Geschichte des Instrumental-Konzerts bis auf die Gegenwart* (Leipzig, 1905; 2nd edition, 1927/R1965)

Schiedermair, L., *Der junge Beethoven* (Bonn and Leipzig, 1925)

Schilling-Trygophorus, O., 'Das Ethos des Klanges in Beethovens Violinkonzert', *Neues Beethoven-Jahrbuch* 5 (1934), pp. 154–8

Schlosser, J. A., *Ludwig van Beethoven* (Prague, 1828)

Schmidt-Görg, J., and Schmidt, H. (eds.), *Ludwig van Beethoven* (London, 1970)

Schmitz, A., *Beethoven* (Bonn, 1927)

Schwarz, B., 'Beethoven and the French Violin School', *Musical Quarterly* 44 (1958), pp. 431–47

Great Masters of the Violin (London, 1984)

French Instrumental Music between the Revolutions (1789–1830) (New York, 1987)

Segerman, E., 'Strings through the Ages', *The Strad* 99 (1988), pp. 52–5, 195–201 and 295–99.

Seyfried, I. von, *Ludwig van Beethovens Studien in General-Basse, Contrapuncte und in der Compositions-Lehre* (Vienna, 1832)

Solomon, M., *Beethoven* (New York, 1977)

Beethoven Essays (Cambridge, Mass., 1988)

Sommers, L., 'Beethoven's Violin Concerto', *Music and Letters* 15 (1934), pp. 46–9

Sonneck, O. G., *Beethoven: Impressions of Contemporaries* (New York, 1926)

Stowell, R. (ed.), *Performing Beethoven* (Cambridge, 1994)

Swain, J. P., 'Form and Function of the Classical Cadenza', *The Journal of Musicology* 6/1 (1988), pp. 27–59

Tovey, D., *Essays in Musical Analysis* (7 vols., London, 1935–9/R1972)
Beethoven (London, 1944)

Tyson, A., 'Beethoven's Heroic Phase', *Musical Times* 110 (1969) pp. 139–41
'The Text of Beethoven's Op. 61', *Music and Letters* 43 (1962), pp. 104–14
'The Textual Problems of Beethoven's Violin Concerto', *Musical Quarterly* 53 (1967), pp. 482–502
The Authentic English Editions of Beethoven (London, 1963)

White, E. C., 'Did Viotti Write Any Original Piano Concertos?', *Journal of the American Musicological Society* 22 (1969), pp. 275–84
'First-movement Form in the Violin Concerto from Vivaldi to Viotti', in T. Noblitt (ed.), *Music East and West: Essays in Honor of Walter Kaufmann* (New York, 1981)
'Form in the Second and Third Movements of the Classical Violin Concerto', *Journal of Musicological Research* 6 (1986), pp. 270–89

Whitmore, P., *Unpremeditated Art – The Cadenza in the Classical Keyboard Concerto* (Oxford, 1991)

Index

122

Index

Eichler, Friedrich Wilhelm, 34–5
Einstein, Alfred, 14, 15
Eliason, Eduard(?), 35
Enesco, Georges, 60

Fétis, François-Joseph, 34
Fischer, Wilfried, 5, 6
Fiske, Roger, 68, 75
Flesch, Carl, 38–9, 40, 43, 45, 95, 100
Förster, Emanuel Aloys, 11
Francescatti, Zino, 40, 98
Furtwängler, Wilhelm, 41, 98

Galamian, Ivan, 41
Gelinek, Abbé Josef, 2
Gesellschaft der Musikfreunde, 4
Gielen, Michael, 42, 99
Goodman, Roy, 42, 98
Grove, Sir George, 75
Grumiaux, Arthur, 40, 98
Gulomy, Jérôme, 34, 35

Habeneck, François-Antoine, 13, 34
Haitink, Bernard, 40, 98, 99
Hanslick, Eduard, 37–8
Harmonicon, The, 35
Harnoncourt, Nikolaus, 41
Haydn, Joseph, 1, 21, 23–4
Heermann, Hugo, 38
Heifetz, Jascha, 40, 95, 98
Hellmesberger, Joseph (Sen.), 5, 93, 100, 109n.14
Herttrich, Ernst, xi, 42
Hess, Willy, 4–5, 6, 43, 55, 114n.45
Hickman, Roger, 80
Hofmann, Leopold, 20
Holz, Karl, 3, 37
Hubay, Jenö, 43, 45, 95–6, 100
Huggett, Monica, 42

Indy, Vincent d', 1

Jacobsen, Maxim, 95, 100
Jahn, Otto, 54, 55
Jander, Owen, x, 75–6, 79–85, 116n.9

Joachim, Joseph, 11, 33, 35–8, 39, 42, 43–4, 45, 46, 68, 94, 95, 100
Jochum, Eugen, 42
Jonas, Oswald, 55

Kaiser, Fritz, 48, 55, 58
Karajan, Herbert von, 42, 98
Kaskin, Nikolai, 39
Kempen, Paul van, 42, 98
Kennedy, Nigel, 97
Klemperer, Otto, 41
Klimov, Valéry, 41
Koch, Heinrich Christoph, 79–80
Kogan, Leonid, 41
Kojima, Shin Augustinus, x, xi, 55, 56–8
Kondrashin, Kirill, 41
Kozeluch, Leopold, 86
Kreisler, Fritz, 40, 43–4, 68, 94–5, 98, 100
Kremer, Gidon, 41, 93
Kreutzer, Rodolphe, 8, 11, 12–13, 14, 17, 18, 19, 23, 111n.1
  Violin Concertos No. 4, 19
    No. 6,   18
    No. 13,   19
    No. 16,   19
Krumpholz, Wenzel, 2, 3, 8, 11
  Abendunterhaltung, 8
Kubelík, Jan, 43–4
Kulenkampff, Georg, 40, 98

Lamoureux, Charles, 38
Lannoy, Eduard von, 37
Laub, Ferdinand, 38, 95, 100
Léonard, Hubert, 95, 100
Lichnowsky, Prince Carl von, 2, 7, 56
Lobkowitz, Prince Joseph, 2

Mackerras, Sir Charles, 42
Manén, Juan, 5, 110n.20
Marriner, Sir Neville, 41
Marteau, Henri, 95
Mayseder, Joseph, 11
Mehta, Zubin, 41
Méhul, Etienne-Nicolas, 14, 30, 111n.1

Index

Mendelssohn, Felix, ix, 11, 35, 36
Menuhin, Yehudi, 40–1, 74, 98
Morning Post, The, 36
Moser, Andreas, 45, 46, 61–2
Moser, Hans Joachim, 75, 80
Möser, Johann Nepomuk, 30–1
Mozart, Leopold, 9–10
Mozart, Wolfgang Amadeus, ix, 1, 4, 15, 20, 24, 30, 61, 68
   cadenzas, 90–1, 93
   violin concertos, ix, 20
Mozart: works
   Violin Concerto K.218,   15
   Piano Concerto K.271,   90
   Sinfonia Concertante K.364,   90
   Piano Concerto K.453,   15, 90
   Piano Concerto K.459,   15
   Piano Concerto K.466,   24
   Piano Concerto K.491,   4
   Piano Concerto K.503,   61
Munch, Charles, 40, 98
Musical World, The, 36
Mutter, Anne-Sophie, 42

Neate, Charles, 49
Nottebohm, Gustav, 54–5, 57
Nováček, Ottakar, 93, 100

Oistrakh, David, 41, 98
Oistrakh, Igor, 41

Paganini, Niccolò, 35, 38
   'Paganini' bowing, 46
Paris, 8, 9, 12, 13, 14, 30, 34, 38, 47
Perlman, Itzhak, 41, 98
Philharmonic Society (London), 33, 35, 36
Pössinger, Alexander, 55
Pugnani, Gaetano, 12

Rasumovsky, Count Andreas, 2
Ricci, Ruggiero, 117n.6
Ries, Ferdinand, 3, 48
Ries, Franz, 3
Rochlitz, Friedrich, 32

Rode, Pierre, 10, 12, 13, 14, 23, 33, 92
romance (*Romanze*), 4, 5, 6, 16, 24, 26, 75, 79, 80, 85
Romberg, Andreas, 11
Romberg, Bernhard, 11
Rosen, Charles, 61
Rostal, Max, 43–4, 93, 101
Rousseau, Jean-Jacques, 80, 81, 85
Rovantini, Franz Georg, 3
Rudolph (Johann Joseph Rainer), Archduke of Austria, 2, 13, 23

Saint-Saëns, Camille, 96, 101
Salieri, Antonio, 1
Salomon, Johann Peter, 21
Sarasate, Pablo de, 38, 43–4
Schauspielhaus an der Wien, 30
Schering, Arnold, 14
Schindler, Anton, 24, 32
Schlemmer, Wenzel, 52
Schneiderhan, Wolfgang, 42, 93, 98, 101
Schmidt-Isserstedt, Hans, 40, 98
Schnittke, Alfred, 41, 97
Schradieck, Henry, 95, 101
Schubert, Franz, 64
Schumann, Clara, 37
Schumann, Robert, 35, 37
Schuppanzigh, Ignaz, 3, 11, 13, 30
Schwarz, Boris, x, 16–17
Seyfried, Ignaz von, 21–2
Singer, Edmund, 95, 101
Sitkovetsky, Dmitri, 41
Smart, Sir George, 3
Société des Concerts du Conservatoire, 34, 38
Solomon, Maynard, 1
Spalding, Albert, 41, 101
Spohr, Louis, ix, 13, 21, 23, 33, 34, 45, 68, 93–4, 101
Steibelt, Daniel, 2, 48
Stern, Isaac, 41, 98
Sulzer, Johann Georg, 79, 80, 85
Süssmayr, Franz Xaver, 21
Swensen, Joseph, 93
Swieten, Baron Gottfried van, 2

Index

Szeryng, Henryk, 40, 98
Szigeti, Joseph, 40, 43, 45, 98, 104

Tennstedt, Klaus, 41, 97, 98
Tetzlaff, Christian, 42, 98
Thayer, Alexander Wheelock, 3, 23
Theater an der Wien, 21
Thomson, César, 43–4
Tomasini, Luigi (Jun.), 34
Tourte, François, 6, 8, 9, 10, 12
Tourte, Louis (père), 8
Tovey, Sir Donald Francis, 5, 50, 61,
  63–4, 75, 92, 96, 101
Triebensee, Josef, 21
Tyson, Alan, x, xi, 49, 51, 52, 53, 54,
  58–9, 102, 103, 105, 107–8, 114n.2,
  115n.11, 116n.8

Uhlrich, Karl Wilhelm, 34
Urakawa, Takaya, 110n.22

Vieuxtemps, Henri, 34, 37, 38, 95–6, 101
Vienna, 1, 2, 3, 4, 8, 9, 10, 11, 12, 13, 20,
  21, 22, 24, 30, 32, 33, 34, 37, 45, 46,
  47, 49, 50, 51, 56, 58
violin (in early nineteenth century), 6–7
Viotti, Giovanni Battista, ix, 8, 9, 10, 12,
  13, 14–15, 16, 17–19, 20, 21, 22, 24,
  47, 48
  Violin Concertos
    No. 1,   18
    No. 5,   17, 18
    No. 6,   18, 19

No. 7,   16
No. 13,   16
No. 22,   ix, 17, 18
No. 23,   16
No. 26,   18
No. 27,   18
No. 28,   18
No. 29,   18

Waldstein, Count Ferdinand, 1
Walter, Bruno, 40, 98
Weber, Carl Maria von, 21
Wegeler, Franz, 1, 47
Weimar Journal des Luxus und der Moden,
  57–8
Westerholt, Count von, 23
Whitmore, Philip, 92
Wiele, Adolf, 32–3
Wiener Zeitung, 50
Wieniawski, Henryk, 38, 95–6
Wilhelmj, August, 5, 43–4, 45, 95, 101
Williams, Peter, x, 67
Winkler, Julius, 96, 101
Winter, Robert, 9
Woelfl, Joseph, 86
Woldemar, Michel, 9
World, The, 39
Wranitzky, Anton, 11

Ysaÿe, Eugène, 20, 36, 38, 39, 43–4,
  95–6, 101

Zukerman, Pinchas, 41

Printed in the United States
74733LV00002B/79-96